Objects in the Rear View Mirror

Edited by: A.J. Huffman

and April Salzano

Cover Art: "I-80" by Nate Dworsky

Copyright © 2015 A.J. Huffman

All rights reserved. Except for brief quotations in critical articles or reviews, no part of this book may be reproduced in any manner without prior written permission from the publisher:

Kind of a Hurricane Press
www.kindofahurricanepress.com
kindofahurricanepress@yahoo.com

CONTENTS

Featured Piece

Len Saculla	*From a Booster Cushion*	11

From the Authors

Jeanne Althouse	*Convertible Girl*	17
Charles Eugene Anderson	*To Whom It May Concern*	19
Allen Ashley	*They Drive by Night*	21
	Bumper Stickers	23
Bob Beagrie	*Road Rage*	25
	Tat Tvam Asi	26
Henri Bensussen	*Reading the Signs*	27
Jane Blanchard	*Untitled*	29
Wayne F. Burke	*Stopped*	30
Jane Burn	*Driving on a Hot Day*	31
Miki Byrne	*The Building of Neverbudge*	32
	The Drive	34
	Roadside Shrine	35
Alan Catlin	*Untitled*	36
Louisa Clerici	*Broken Radio*	38
Darren Colbourne	*Night Rush*	39
Esteban Colon	*Screaming through Car Speakers*	41

	A Tourists Guide to Driving in Chicago	42
	Snapshots	43
Jeff Coomer	*Who was the Best Man at Your Wedding?*	45
Betsey Cullen	*Consummation*	46
Mark Danowsky	*Bad Trouble Finds a Face*	47
Emer Davis	*With a Disco in My Head*	48
Lenny DellaRocca	*Fetish*	49
	A Good Cup of Coffee	50
Andrea Janelle Dickens	*Returning*	51
E.M. Eastick	*Skeleton Coast*	52
Delaine Fragnoli	*Dropping at Dusk through the Curves*	54
Diane Gage	*The Fault in Our Cars*	55
Patricia L. Goodman	*Driving Home*	57
	On the Way Home	58
John Grey	*I'm Leaving Morristown Forever*	59
Barbara Gurney	*Rust*	61
Kevin M. Hibshman	*Driving as if in a Dream*	62
Aaron E. Holst	*Driving I-15 South of Dillon, MT, Middle of Night, Playing an Alphabet Game to Stay*	63

Ruth Holzer	Driving It Home	65
Ann Howells	Liebchen	66
	Right Turn at Calloway	67
	Friday Rush Hour	69
Liz Hufford	Rider Remorse	71
Diane Jackman	Homesickness	72
Steve Klepetar	Empty Highway	73
	Road Map	74
	Getting Lost in My Own Town	75
Natalie Korman	A Gas Station in Van Meter, Iowa	76
Pat M. Kuras	White Horse Beach Dream	77
Ron. Lavalette	Revisiting Venus	78
Mary Masaba	The Parking Space	79
Amanda M. May	To the End of the Unending Road	82
Sharon Lask Munson	Silence Fills the Car	85
	Parking Rules	87
	Driving	89
Carol Murphy	Road Kill	90
Liz Tynes Netto	The Crossing	93
	Boy Soldiers	94
James B. Nicola	It's Time	96

ayaz daryl nielsen	Untitled	97
Amy S. Pacini	Memory's Eye	98
Carl Palmer	Residential Road Rage	100
Andrew Periale	Pudelnaß	101
	Storm Driver	102
Richard King Perkins II	Aprilville	103
Lisa Reinhardt	Prison	104
Gillie Robic	Remote Control	105
Karen Sylvia Rockwell	Travelling East at Sundown	106
Ilene H. Rudman	Motor Oil	107
Ed Schelb	The Aladdin Lamp Company	108
	Elegy for a Buick Skylark	111
Wendy L. Schmidt	On a Wheel and a Prayer	113
Carol A. Stephen	Stupid Things to Think About While Driving	115
David Subacchi	Triumph 2000	116
Marianne Szlyk	Travels with the White Ghost	118
	Thelma at the Beach	120
	The Poet Charlotte Drives Away	121
Susan Tally	From this Day Forward	123
Barbara Tate	The Coward's Road	124

Tim Tobin	The Bridge to Somewhere	125
Jack Turner	Undesignated Driver	127
Jessica Van de Kemp	To the Ocean	132
John Vicary	The Rearview	133
Michelle Villanueva	Blank Revelry	135
Connie Walle	Department of Licensing	136
Mercedes Webb-Pullman	Some Days You're Just Angry	137
Ron Yazinski	Little Rock to Memphis	139
Cliff Young	Momentum	140
Ellen Roberts Young	American Dreaming	143
Fred Zirm	Du Temps Perdu	144
	Parallel Parking	145

From the Editors

A.J. Huffman	Highway Chess	149
	The I-4 Parking Lot	150
	Of Cars	151
	Sun Through a Car Window	152
	A Strange Scraping	153
	My Tire Had a Nipple	154
	My Niece Threatened to Piss	155
	When Cars Look Like Stars	156

	The Trouble with Family Road Trips	157
April Salzano	In the Car	159
	Mazephobia	160
	Last Night I Ran Over My Autistic Son	161
	Poem for a Phobia	162
	1980 Pontiac Sunbird	163
	1987 Cutlass Calais	164
	1997 Saturn Sedan	165
	1998 Nissan Sentra	166
	2012 Jeep Liberty	167
	Author Bios	171
	About the Editors	187

Featured Piece

This anthology's featured piece represents the editors' choice for the best artistic interpretation of the theme of Cars and Driving, and for that reason, the editors feel it deserves special focus.

From A Booster Cushion

I was a precocious four-year-old. I'd been for a sleepover with Danny whom I'd met at kindergarten. We'd become friends because his parents kept tortoises, hamsters, tropical fish and a couple of somnolent dogs. I was animal crazy – picture books, DVDs, zoo brochures. I knew the names of hundreds of creatures.

Now my Dad had picked me up and was driving me off to my Grandma's where I'd be staying for the weekend. I didn't use the child's car seat anymore. Instead, I had a booster cushion which helped give me a view out of the window.

The wasps were busy tonight. Always in a hurry, cutting corners, narrowing angles, you'd see them briefly pass you then they were away swift and carefree along the dark road.

Daddy had his Lynx deodorant on. I knew he was going to see Shelley, my new stepmum, after he'd dropped me off. His hands on the steering wheel were clean and his shirt cuffs freshly ironed.

Suddenly a silver Toyota cut in front of us, crossing from the outside land and only just making the turn-off.

"Idiots!" Dad cursed.

But they weren't idiots; it was a pair of slavering hyenas within the vehicle.

So then I shouted, "Daddy, daddy, can't you see? The cars are all being driven by animals!"

"What, Jason? Oh yeah, I get it, the way they're behaving… yeah, I make you right there, son."

I was smart for my age but I wasn't yet in the habit of applied metaphor.

"No, Daddy, look! There's a tiger behind that wheel and the truck's being driven by an elephant."

Horns blaring. Or should that have been horns and tusks and antlers all extended? We swerved viciously, narrowly avoiding a high-speed collision. Father swore, apologised for his language then turned both barrels on me to pipe down in the back, I was getting dangerous.

I was getting dangerous? The motorway now was like the great migration and, outside our metal and glass bubble, there was not a human to be seen. It was like someone had said Noah's Ark is open for business, first come first served, and this had led to a veritable flood of traffic headed for salvation. Or something better.

Just as quickly as it had surfaced, my vision faded. The world was back to normal. Even the back-up caused by the airport turn-off and the consequent logjam of traffic didn't change us all into bleating sheep. Just ordinary people: tired commuters, holidaymakers, day trippers, truckers and salesmen, power-dressed women off to marketing meetings. Just the occasional child of my age or a bit older, greeting my presence with a shy wave.

But there was one further twist. A guy in a black sports car cut us up just as we turned onto the residential streets of Northton. He had red fire flashes painted along the bodywork like he was a fire-breathing dragon. My father, enraged, sped up and overtook the would-be dragster, completing a smart maneuver that forced the man to brake sharply with a squeal and a screech. Dad popped his seatbelt clip and opened the door in one fluid motion. I was astonished that he was able to exit the vehicle successfully because suddenly he was a huge bear, angered by a bee sting, claws extended, ready to swipe at all obstacles in his path. I squirmed around on my booster cushion, fearful at what was about to occur and expecting, given the flames decorating his vehicle, a fierce dragon to emerge from the other car. Instead, I saw a pinch-faced weasel, a cowering creature against my father's ursine wrath. I couldn't discern every accusation but the gist was, unsurprisingly, that Dad had a little one in the car and didn't greatly appreciate idiots putting our lives in peril.

As I watched, the two verbal combatants morphed back from their hidden natures into normal human form. It ended with a handshake and all-round apology.

"You all right, little guy?" Dad asked.

"Sure. When will we get to Grandma's?"

"Soon now."

-- Len Saculla

From The Authors

Convertible Girl

He left me. Forsaken. For a younger model. Tears of shock, rage, and hurt flooded my abandoned heart. I told myself: so what if she has a power tilt-and-slide moon roof, I am, after all, one of the first open airs. But that didn't help. I was devastated.

When I was young, I was small but I had a big engine and he said he loved that about me. How could he so easily forget those Saturday mornings when, parked in the garage, I pleasured him while he lay grinning below me? I knew he Googled other models in secret, but I thought he would be faithful to the end. He was always close with his money, said driving a new one off the lot cost thousands of dollars and wasn't worth it, even if they did get better mileage.

Age took me completely by surprise. I couldn't believe it when my tail pipe sagged, my muffler broke, and my exhaust had issues which caused me to fail inspection. I suffered two tire replacements with complications. When I looked at my reflection in the garage door, I noticed the corners of the front grill had settled into wrinkles that gave me a tired look and at night my headlights had a vacant stare. It couldn't be me; inside I still felt brand new.

He complained that I couldn't rev up as much as I used to. My odometer conked out and after that he looked openly at other cars. Then he fell in love with Cherry—a red-hooded hybrid with a remote keyless ignition system. Frankly she's an immature youngster who can't commit to either gas or electric, but all he talked about to the salesman as he traded me in was the miracle of that smart key. Angry, embittered, I told myself his outrageous trophy-love wouldn't last. I was old, but he was older. Six decades plus and she was a mere teen.

He drove off with Cherry and abandoned me on the used car lot. I was stolen by a drug dealer who only wanted the money from my viable parts. When the thief took me to be assessed at Old

Ride, where they offered "Classic Car Parts for Sale", the manager wanted me and took me off his hands for a few hundred.

My new owner towed me to the Car Spa where they gave me a valve job, replaced my upholstery, and restored the lost waterproofing to my top. With the golden glow I developed from his restoration, his fingers tuning my engine, the massage of the spray paint, and the exercise possible with new tires, I became worthy of a jaunt around town, although I have to stick to under 25 m.p.h.

I'll never forget the first Saturday morning he took me out for a drive. Young men, working half-day at a neighborhood construction site, whistled when we passed; that hadn't happened in years. When we parked at his favorite coffee shop, his friends leaned over my open window. They stared at my polished dash and peeked underneath my newly-oiled leather seats. With all their attention, my owner purred as loud as my rebuilt engine.

My ex saw me and wants me back. Says he's going to divorce his hybrid, couldn't communicate with the navigation system, complains the steering is all wrong, a floating feeling at every green light, hates having to engage the power button on the ramp to the freeway. Cherry doesn't remember the good old days before there were computers running cars and the two of them don't have anything to talk about. He confessed he misses the car key and poking it in and out of my ignition.

My ex offered an exorbitant price, but, thank God, my new owner wouldn't sell. He said I am a classic open air and I am irreplaceable.

-- Jeanne Althouse

To Whom It May Concern

Vanguard Aeronautical
Palo Alto, California 94310

To Whom It May Concern:

I have bought many cars over the years, and all of them have been ground cars. Ever since I was a young man, I have always dreamed of owning a flying car. I finally decided to buy one when your company offered the promotional flying lessons rebate.

I was really happy the day I passed my FAA exam, and I received my Class FC license.

My neighbors were jealous when the dealership delivered the black model ILC 500 I ordered. Martin Jones, who lives next door, actually slammed his front door when he saw my new car land in my driveway, and I haven't seen him since. I felt such euphoria when I heard muffled cursing from behind his entry. I think he slammed his door so hard it actually scared a small flock of finches living in the maple tree in front of his house.

My wife saw my happiness from the kitchen window, and she was really pleased with the terms of the four year lease I was able to secure.

Unfortunately, I did have more difficulty at the dealership with the finance manager who kept insisting I should purchase the clear coat finish package, and the air-intake protectors. I said to him, 'if it was so important then the FAA would've required it on every flying car.' That shut him up, but I did end up buying the clear coat package.

Who knew my first flight would be my last one? I slowly lifted off from my driveway and everything seemed to be going a-okay. The turbo fans of the engine increased revolutions, but it seemed like it was smooth and safe.

Okay, I was just hoping for a quick flight around the neighborhood so I could show off a little bit. After I waved goodbye to my wife, I have to admit I flew my car a little too close to the ground, just above the tree tops. But I was really happy, and the whole sky opened up before my windshield. It was truly beautiful.

Afterwards everything went wrong, the heads-up computer showed a fire in the starboard turbo fan, and my car started to spin to the ground. Luckily on impact, the side airbags saved my life. I crashed landed the car, and it turned sideways and hit Martin's tree. Fortunately, I was able to walk away from the crash with only a few scratches, and a dislocated shoulder. However, the small population of finches in my neighborhood were not so fortunate, as many of them had been sucked through my flying car's turbofan where they were incinerated in the afterburner.

My ILC 500 was declared a total loss by my insurance company, and the FAA found I was at fault for not attaining the proper altitude in a residential neighborhood.

I am still recovering from my shoulder injury, and my wife insists I ride with her in our old ground car for the time being. I also have to take the FAA suspended FC license course, and attend a week's worth of classes from the State of Colorado on better understanding the rights of our wildlife friends. Yet, once my insurance check comes through, I know I will purchase another ILC 500, but next time I will make sure it includes all of the recommended safety features, and I will yield to the charm of finches.

Sincerely,
Chuck Anderson
Denver, Colorado 80218

-- Charles Eugene Anderson

They Drive By Night

Pylon, pylon, pylon, bridge,
light, light, light, lay-by,
roadsign, roadsign, roadsign, turn-off
not taken.

World reduced to nocturnal tunnel:
ill-lit by sodium or coned headlamps,
repetitive features,
featureless.
Tiny, metal-shelled creatures
on endless metalled roads
unloved and less-travelled
at this hour.

Light, roadsign, light, pylon;
lay-by, hard shoulder, grass verge.

On all sides around you only dark matter,
the unknown presence
the theory that there is a world
beyond this internal combustion capsule:
a place we think we once came from
and to which we may yet return.

Pylon, pylon, discarded traffic cones;
even the Sat-Nav's fallen silent.
Memories of her regular request to
"Perform a U-turn where possible" bring a
smile to your face.

Motorway, highway, autobahn, grand rue.

Radio station sends its signals through the night air
playing oldies, sing-along standards of yesteryear
like the time capsule stowed on "Voyager"
or the transmissions that head inexorably

to the light-year distant stars.
So you turn to a talk station
but even the news of the day –
wars, sports scores, celebrities celebrating themselves –
seems somehow anachronistic,
bland by age,
irrelevant in this existence:
echoes from an expired Earth.

Light, light, light not working,
light orange; light whitish.
How many hours now? How much
                              further?

Grass bank. Hedge. Tattered trees.
Light, pylon, light, roadsign.
Decreasing chevrons, roadsign, roadsign, turn-off
taken.

                -- Allen Ashley

Bumper Stickers

"My other car's a Porsche"
Well, no, actually it's a beaten-up pair
of Puma plimsolls
for when this beast won't start in the mornings
– that's most mornings –
and I have to jog into the office
like a Muppet.

"Toot if you got some last night"
Got some what? Sex
most obviously.
Chance would be
a fine thing.
But feel free to toot
if you got some fries
or pizza
or a couple of Buds
or even, just this once, some sleep.

"Don't Follow Me, Follow The Tornadoes"
I think they might be a sports team –
football or basketball,
something with rapid movement in it
unlike this pile of junk.
Maybe they mean real tornadoes, though,
like in that film "Twister".
Or "White Tornado", which is something
you shove down the toilet;
which is what I'd like to do with this rust-bucket.

"Supplied by Osborne Motors, Diagnostic Specialists"
Like they're doctors or some such!
Shysters.
They couldn't diagnose a punch in the gut.
Yeah I paid them in cash.
Paperwork's all valid for another two months:

make me an offer.
I can't refuse.

                -- Allen Ashley

Road Rage

Inflated by the back-draught
a pair of green workmen's
gloves crawl through the slush
of the middle lane of the A19,
Northbound, the left vanishes
beneath my undercarriage,
the other, I see in my rear
view mirror, rolls over onto
its back to give me the finger.

-- Bob Beagrie

Tat Tvam Asi

The *something* about those long car journeys
after the fluster of departure and we'd settled
into the route and a comfortable quietude
and I could stare out of the window at a tree
in a field with its shadow, the line of a hillside
the folds of the moors under the raw clouds
a greened boulder in the swell of heather,
though the seeing was more like the tasting
of a fresh nettle leaf complete with its sting
an ingesting that tugged me out of the car, out
of the body of the boy I was and into the thing
that was held within its solid, particular wonder
as if the Radio DJ had begun to chant 'This Art
Thou' as we passed on our way to *elsewhere*.

-- Bob Beagrie

Reading the Signs

Frosted sheep in frosted pastures
face east to thaw under a fat morning sun.

Highway flashing signs: Icy Roads
and Don't Text While Driving, Fines

Are Not Worth It. Spring wonder
of rockslides, splintered bull pines.

Ophthalmologist at noon, Dr. Mason:
left eyelid, stye entrenched, walled in.

Four months of treatment, call it a draw
like in Iraq, Iran, Afghanistan. Rebel

takeover of oil gland. *Sometimes
they go away on their own*, he says

*or turn cancerous—happened once
in my experience.* I glance at my arm.

Last week my surgeon called:
Thought you'd want to know I got it all.

On the face, between shoulder blades,
the arm a rutted country road of mole removal.

Turning back, the same curvaceous
highway, green ferns and firs and wild

ginger, sheep on their feet now, grazing
ewes and lambs not yet shorn, I ease up

for the slow approach, accelerate out,
coast, brake in time to meet the next one

like swimming against a riptide
pulling in air before the waves hit.

-- Henri Bensussen

torrential rainfall
visibility reduced
car washed if not wiped

      -- Jane Blanchard

Stopped

Had a headlight out
and got stopped
by a cop
who politely and unnecessarily
introduced himself as
he shined his light
on my expired inspection sticker
then asked for my license
which I gave him,
but not my insurance card
which I could not find,
and he went away
then returned
and said my license had expired too
and he asked me to step out of the car
into the street
where I stood
exposed in the glare of headlights
and I wondered
what else
I had not been
paying attention to.

-- Wayne F. Burke

Driving on a Hot Day

Liquid heat sheen blisters above sizzling tarmac.
Squint-eyed against the sun, it's like my car can walk
on water - it's like driving into melted air, like finding
a rend in the sky's fabric and passing through it.

Foral turpentine aftertaste from the sticky bag of sweeties
on the dash. I am breathing daisies, singing dog-rose out
along with some song on the radio. Someone is bound
to make that joke about frying eggs on pavements.

The wheels scatter bone-dry horse shit as if it was
feathered breath. The air is hot and heavy - greenhouse,
vegetation. It is almost as if I am steering blind into
silver ribbons. The road is a ripple and I am afloat.

-- Jane Burn

The Building of Neverbudge

She grew in our weedy back yard.
Formed through rose-bay willow herb,
catmint, dandelions.
Emerged from foraging trips to scrap yards,
binges of slow gathering.
Axles, engine, chassis, frame,
assembled like some dark paleontology.
Headlights, handles, bits and bobs
hoarded in old towels. Smeared in Vaseline
to preserve their silvery chrome,
protect against damp.
The sparky flicker of welders flame
brightened tea-times. Flickered lightning
blue flashes over our sausage and mash,
as Da worked. Greasily smeared, smiling,
forehead furrowed.
Old Commando beret jauntily perched,
fag quirked in the corner of his mouth.
Every weekend, long evenings of summer,
saw his hands twist. Tools, extensions of his arms.
She had two seats. Unpainted bodywork.
Pale aluminum shell, more cockpit than car.
Rivet heads stood proud, like boils on her skin.
She echoed the lines of a Morgan
without the panache. Da tinkered, pottered.
Blissfully oblivious, overalls an insult to hygiene.
A second skin of oil and sweat, banned from the kitchen,
left curled by the door till next day.
Finished, she was too broad for the entry.
Sat marooned in an island of stamped-down grass,
muddy compressed ground.
Neatly spoked wheels up on bricks.
Till neighbors gathered like pallbearers,
to hoist her onto shoulders, turn her sideways.
March her down to the street.
To sit at the curb.

Running-board nudging pavement.
A draw for us kids, the passing milkman.
In a parody of launching Da poured stout over her.
"I name thee Neverbudge." We cheered.
Her engine sparked at first turn of the key.

-- Miki Byrne

The Drive

The roof rack whistles.
We speed toward his dream.
This journey is for his resurrection,
not ours.
Miles are covered.
Eaten by wheel-spun revolutions.
Memories ooze from him.
Time folds as pages of unhappiness
are turned, turned again.
Until their edges fray and he stops,
weeps as we sit in the back seat.
Silent, afraid.
As he tells himself, it will be alright now.

-- Miki Byrne

Roadside Shrine

He is not here.
On this bleak curve.
Where you leave flowers.
Shed swift tumbling tears.
He is gone.
Removed from this place
where he fell. Unprotected.
To scream into the night.
Lit red by that hit and run's retreat.
He does not linger at the roadside.
Tainted by exhaust,
Ignored by streams of traffic.
Wrapped by wind-whipped litter.
Do not tend a trough
of dusty plants here,
or hang a ribbon in the hedgerow.
Go to where you loved him best.
Take him home.

-- Miki Byrne

> *"Fasten your seat belts, it's going to be a bumpy night."*
>
> -- Bette Davis in "All About Eve"

Their latest epic drunk began in a bar
on Central Avenue a few doors down
from Quail.
"What side of the road are we on?"
"Left, heading East."
"Left it is. Last time we did all the bars
on the right side of Western heading East
and never made it out of town."
The instigator woke in the back room
of a bar somewhere in Troy, unsure whether
it was day or night, looking up into
the face of a washed out, formerly-blonde
woman of indeterminate age asking him,
"Got a couple of bucks? We need some
money for some shots and the juke.
The bartender has been giving us funny looks.
I think he's getting nervous."
"Can't imagine why."
"Me neither. Maybe we should just blow this
joint. Keep on heading North."
"You got any matches?"
"Course I do. What do you take me for?"
A question he thought about for a moment,
wisely deciding not to answer.
'What about him?"
"Leave him a couple of bucks and some butts.
He'll be all right."
"Suppose so. Not like it will be the first time
he woke up in a strange bar."
"Or the last."
"Who's driving?"
"You are, wild man, you the one with the car."
"Guess so. Hard part is remembering which
one it is and where it's parked."

"Press that automatic key thing. It'll find itself."
"A drunk man's best friend."
"Ain't it the truth."
"Where we headed?"
"North."
North in misting rain, no visibility on winding
back roads by the overflowing creek swollen
with snowmelt runoff from the hills somewhere
down a culvert studded with bare trees.

-- Alan Catlin

Broken Radio

I drive by the lake every day,
notice smoky white snow
just kissing the shore with ice.

I fly right past
thinking some day, far away,
I will stop and go for a swim.

My radio is broken
but no silence fills the car.
I am convinced I am not alone.

She sits with me on the grass, red lipstick, soggy flip-flops.
We peer at the ducks under the bridge,
offer them remnants of bacon-egg sandwiches.

The leaves of the maple tree are blue and orange,
have stripes and yellow polka-dots, in my dreams anything goes.
I swim in the lake, cold as snow and she is still with me.

-- Louisa Clerici

Night Rush

I still sing 'em ragged for you and Maria/We don't drive nowhere without the radio on"

– Angry Johnny and the Radio

I spend my nights on curves
That I like to take hard and fast,
The turbo zipping along to the rhythm
Of the bumblebees in my honeycomb thoughts;
Structured but hollowed out,
Highways of chaotic dissonance.
Gaslight plays on the radio,
Songs about Audrey Hepburn,
Girls in party dress.
Upshift and foot down,
Power back downshift as wheels slide out,
Eyes and knees lock,
The bees now swimming bloodstream back-roads
Down my arms and
Into vibrating hands.
Miles later my eyes open
To the sky of a spectral audience,
The heat of the engine warming
My back through the hood,
I feel like a kid in the 50's
Watching and waiting
For the bomb to fall,
The starting line is twenty years back
And I think the finish
Is around a dark corner
Cut a bit too close;
But I'll be damned if I don't love the noise in between,
So I roll off the hood
Onto my feet
And strap back in
Because the roads tie together

The darkness of empty nights and besides:
The radio is on.

-- Darren Colbourne

Screaming through Car Speakers

low hanging eyes
cry through a lead foot
engine
        roar replacing drywall breaking knuckles.

-- Esteban Colon

A Tourist's Guide to Driving in Chicago

1. You have the right of way.
                                           I don't care what they taught you in Driver's Ed
       the right of way is yours . . .
                                                             at all times.

2. If someone pulls a weapon on you,   drive off
       even if "off" means you have to drive on the sidewalk.

3. The police have better things to do than harass you, unless you hit someone
              or stop traffic around you

4. If someone does something that makes no sense,
                                                   remember
       half the people on the road around you are drunk

5. Don't be offended by anything another driver says,
                       most of these assholes think they have the right of way.

                            -- Esteban Colon

Snapshots

                                                                (Vs)

- bright

flash of closed eyes. Pain like a younger brother flailing arms,
begging the rest of the world wait.

- sound like violence, the scream of rubber

tied to the stake.

- aerial ballet, his

thin legs signaling victory
as if to distract us from a twisted torso
shoulder and face
finding glass so quickly, it cracks
to frame them

- shocked strangers

vocabularies stripped down to pained vowels

- twenty

feet above, the summer sky paints a pristine planet,
frozen to watch

- Hands

threatening to squeeze through the steering wheel, he
cycles prayer and profanity
out a record skip mouth

- abandoned

clothes on the ground, his form twists
like Christmas lights in storage,   backdrop
thick and red

- chart
an hour later, reads: "Car vs Pedestrian"
as machines beep

                like his own shallow breaths

-- Esteban Colon

Who was the Best Man at Your Wedding?

In high school there wasn't a back road
within 50 miles he and I didn't cruise
the length of in the late hours of a Friday night,
earnestly sorting out each other's lives while
listening to the music that still defines us,
or sometimes letting the songs alone
do that difficult work. Once we drove
all the way to Philadelphia, two states
and 100 miles distant, before either of us
said anything; then on the trip back our banter
made a row of fast food counter girls laugh
until their manager strolled by to ask
whether he could be of any assistance.
A few nights one of us cried in the other's presence,
an act which in that age of hard men
should have forged a bond between us
as sacred and strong as if we'd clasped cut palms
to mingle blood. Neither of us had much use
for such rituals back then, but now
I'd have gladly taken up a knife and more
to keep our lives from coming to this –
my face just a speck in his rear-view mirror,
his name the secret answer a credit card company
is waiting for me to type.

-- Jeff Coomer

Consummation

It's a boy's business—a mating game
to spread sheet specs: dimensions, chassis, fuel
efficiency, gadgets geared to woo, to collude
in courtship. Salesmen fill your dance card.
Feel her corner. Respond to touch. Accelerate.
Ride smooth. Hug the road. Hear her purr.

Mate chosen, you dicker -- *How much? What's*

the bottom line? Can I drive her home today?

(Can you dampen desire, leave her behind?)

Deal done, flush with success and well spent,
you settle in behind the wheel, power up
the new navigation system. In an instant
she finds her voice, tells you where to go.

-- Betsey Cullen

Bad Trouble Finds a Face

We drove around
in spite of the police
knowing us by name

Lightness of being
meant high, listening
to good albums

If you had a car
you got a job
as a delivery driver

At least cars
were still around
with backseats

Diago began the trend
of yelling drive-by horrors
like "Death-comes-on-swift-wings"

In the car or not
when Diago would cat call
...we stayed silent

-- Mark Danowsky

With a Disco in My Head

My white kandoura lounges
easily into the blackness,
your soft skin creases
as I seep into your crevices,
and follow your unending curves.
Cruising passed zebra crossings,
Music blaring, a two seater
plunged into this sandy cityscape,
encased in your shell,
my fingers tapping the steering wheel,
a carousel of street lamps
Pulsating to the beat.
Shrouded in darkness
and your sultry fumes,
amber lights drifting in the distance,
with a disco in my head,
you are my muse,
a gleaming shadow accelerating
through the night.

-- Emer Davis

Fetish

Every Saturday morning
she goes down to the racetrack,
on hands and knees
in the pit stop, nose to skid marks,
then she goes over to the salvage yard where
a junkyard dog follows her
through teen wreckage,
vehicle after vehicle.
She sniffs Goodyears, Michelins.
She sits at the rear-ends of Mustangs,
old 409s, head against T-Bird whitewalls.
The Doberman pricks his ears with
each gasp and sigh.
She rubs a hand around the rims
of a rusted Edsel, fingers brush gently
over the hard stems of New Yorkers.
Her breath shallow, palms sweat.
Butterflies in her stomach
like the first time a driver kissed her belly
behind the stadium at the track
during the figure eight
transistor radio playing *Brown-Eyed Girl*.
She sticks her fingertip in the hole,
closes her eyes, slowly lets air out,
bobs her head, sucks, sniffs
until firmness goes soft.
Satisfied, she leaves but come
Saturday night she's back
jonesin' real good for the plump ones
on that smashed-up '69 Chevelle.

-- Lenny DellaRocca

A Good Cup of Coffee

While making coffee, I see the digital 4:48 a.m. on the microwave oven – amber hieroglyphic glowing in a machine. Someday when I can no longer remember how to drive home from the grocery store, it will accidentally slip out, incontinence of speech, and I'll tell the cop who has pulled me over for driving in the wrong direction down a one-way street *it's 4:48 a.m.* What I will mean, what will have gotten lost on the way to my tongue is: *I must get home.* I must make a good cup of black coffee in a white, porcelain cup because it means more than she can imagine, this young woman who believes she has a long way to go to be me. She just smiles. I stare up at those mirrored sunglasses. There are two of me, one in each lens; both of us speechless.

-- Lenny DellaRocca

Returning

Somewhere in Indiana and still two hours
south of home, I practice apologies to you. The trip
drags on. The land's too flat and wears the story

of glacial retreat. Here, nothing casts shadows
and the sky sags blue; fields hoard their gold
turned ashen, corn harvested five months ago.

The fields reflect the face I imagine you wearing,
lips pursed to withstand Midwestern gales. On the north
horizon, the wind turbines appear. My bus drones on.

I turn to show you, catch myself, sink back
to stare, imagining myself out there alone with them,
stray winter wheat to gild my path among that field

rooted with statues, their churning, choreographed
arms that loll. A turbine near the road
hangs still, one blade stopped perpendicular

to the ground, two arms extended to the sky. A warm
embrace in a frozen land that leads me to doubt
I can expect such greeting when I arrive at home.

-- Andrea Janelle Dickens

Skeleton Coast

Ghost ships and pirates and spirits of sailors,
Haunting the beaches, collecting their souls.
The gates to hell, the guidebook claims.
Hot and bored, I stare at the same and agree.

Corrugations shake me, wake me,
make me wish we'd taken the inland road.
Greyness, flatness, an elusive ocean,
infusing the dust with its soft briny smell.

A hidden car park tucked in the dunes.
Scorching sunlight searing my eyeballs,
even behind sunglasses, under a cap.
Boring into my back, burning my arms.

One of thousands of wrecks,
steel and wood. An intriguing tale, I'm sure,
but in searing heat, a pile of junk.
Unimpressed and wet with sweat, a quick photo will do.

Back in the car, the empty road jars
my spine and needles my nerves.
Maybe I'll die in the land God made in anger,
a prayer to mechanical experts of Hertz.

No traffic today, not a single other car
out this far from civilization.
The landscape changes.
Bumps rise to mounds rise to red mountain ranges.

The setting sun and sign of a junction.
A campervan rattles past in the opposite direction.
Where do they think they're going?
At this time of day, down the road of gray and nothing.

They're probably saying the same about us.
Alas, onward we drive, alive and enlightened.
Level gravel, easier travel,
goodbye Skeleton Coast.

-- E.M. Eastick

Dropping at Dusk through the Curves

We are dropping at dusk through the curves
that will take us down to Pulga bridge
across the Feather River into the canyon

proper. I am probably going too fast
on the way back from Chico I just want
to get home. Around a left-hand corner

a fawn presents itself, unexpectedly.
I hesitate. Then try to do too much
at once I hit the brakes anticipate

how the deer will bolt throw a hand across
my daughter's body. The curve is banked,
it wants to pitch me to the inside.

I do what I should not — cross the double
yellow line. I think hard. I swerve back.
The deer is rooted in place.

My mind's eye can see it all — the tumbling
body, the torn limbs, crush of bone —
But there is just this: a soft thump

from deep within the car's belly. I feel
nothing underneath my wheels. Later
I will check the front bumper, and find it

bloodless. There is nowhere to pull over.
I look in my rearview mirror. I swear
I see the fawn standing, still, in red tail light.

Across the bridge along the river's edge
I tell her this. She does not need to know

I killed that deer for her.

-- Delaine Fragnoli

The Fault in Our Cars

In the beginning, rat-colored Valerie Valiant, shredded cloth dangling from her metal interior roof, just the vehicle for push-starting to a wedding, or for trying to out-shout tire whine all across baked Nebraska: "Lord! Send a revival! Looord, send a re-vi-eye-val -- & let it begin with MEEEEEE!!!"

& good ol' Fuck You Fury! Broken down before we could get out of town, groaning her blues on the crumbling curb. Still, we got where we were going, somehow, eventually.

Once upon a time for awhile there was a beauty, a white '62 T-Bird gift from Dad, totaled in seconds by a drunk. A mirage of a car. A flash bulb. Blinding for an instant then gone, leaving behind blinking spots in front of our eyes.

Afterwards there was that big fishy sashaying V8 tuna boat with chapped black vinyl top-do and room to play croquet in her wide prairie booty boot, queen of the freeway hill, fearless of semis, parked like a whale next to the little red pilotfish MG my sister used to drive, when it was operational.

Amidst a blurred smudge of boring okayish whatevers, often in need of repair, hard to find in parking lots of similars, came vintage sports cars, on their way to fixed-up tricked-out nirvana, or so our son promised, when pressed. Meanwhile, parts lay scattered on the driveway, tinkering chattering pals clustered like bees, oil stains blossomed, engines roared, batteries charged, each car always in serious need of expensive paint. I confess I helped him buy that first red MR2. Such a deal!

One day I took my new inheritance money down to a used car lot and bought you a nice white newish Toyota, to replace the rusty beater you were driving into the ground. We donated the unsellable clunker to charity, but soon you drove the new one across the whole country to live a life you'd been steadily building for yourself without us.

My sister gave me a car she had acquired at the top of her corporate game, pretty Fifi the Camry who leaves a little puddle after using the AC. I get her detailed once a year, treat her right, keep her in the garage. Our son ordered a shiny new Scion all the way from Japan, washed it often and long, fussed over every stray bit of fluff that dared settle for a moment on its precious special skin and eventually drove off in it to his new life north of here.

The last of his MR2s hunkers under a torn tan cover in my garage, still with split leather seats, still frosted unevenly with patchy old paint. Dark green? Dark blue? Some shade of black? I never could tell. For awhile he left parked out front a lesser silverish vehicle, neglecting and ignoring its accumulating corrosive bird poop, dead leaves, dust and mud around tires damming gutter runoff. One frantic visiting weekend he sold it to a pair of brothers before flying back to his job, relationship, adult life elsewhere.

Now Fifi and I brood in our respective parking spaces, wondering where it all went, what it all meant - cool, minimally mobile, and deaf to the fading siren calls of motion, power, speed, horizons. What's the panic? What's the hurry? Where y'all going?

-- Diane Gage

Driving Home

Clouds in low layers
    close enough
for power line poles to poke
        holes in, let the sky fall through.

A car's sudden brake lights –
      the car in front of him
 plows into the snow-mush of the median.
In my rearview
      a spray-fan of slush;
the driver stops, steps out,
        hazards blinking.

A roadside sign to
      Slaughter Beach….

At home, my adult son,
   undergoing radiation to kill his cancer,
is determined to rid my bird feeders
     of grackles,
sent me a photo of himself sitting
 at my deck window, air gun at his shoulder.

Two weeks ago we rejoiced together
       at the end of Christmas.
Now the family rallies
       around their newly fallen brother,

so that next summer we
       can all assemble on vacation,
passing Blackbird Creek
      along the way.

                -- *Patricia L. Goodman*

On the Way Home

Gender violence is the topic
on the radio as I pull onto the highway
in my little red SUV. It is dusk,

but I know the road. I'll be home soon.
I'm startled by a roar of mufflers—
a souped-up Ram pickup looms

in my rearview. Black as its diesel exhaust
it leers through triple LED headlights,
visors pulled down, hooding the windshield.

As I pull up to a light, hands trembling,
it swaggers up beside me.
I hear heavy breathing, laced with

carbon monoxide, as it towers over me,
twin stainless steel mufflers rising
like horns behind the cab.

Lifted on super-sized tires, heavy-duty
struts it could crawl over me, pin
me down. No place to hide, I reach

for my pepper spray, feign interest
in my dashboard until the light
changes and I floor it, escape.

Attack thwarted, the menace veers
into the corner bar to pursue
the hot little silver number

vamping in the parking lot.

-- Patricia L. Goodman

I'm Leaving Morristown Forever

How easily the skin comes off
with the picking
and the flakes of me
depart my flesh
with just the merest brush of wind.

The dust does it,
the hairs that
fall from my comb,
so why not me and
my new Ford,
slick and black,
leather bucket seats,
country stations loaded
in the radio's chamber
peeling off this town.

The things I want to do
need highways,
infrastructure that can differentiate
here from there,
can suck me out of
the way it's always been.

I want advice from blacktop,
from speed, from accelerator conversation,
something new every breath, every second,
the turns, the straightaways,
hitch-hiking mountains
and green-fevered stands of pine,
the dash-board insight,
and the four-lane point of view,
even the cars that zip towards me
going in the same direction,
that out of here
that strips neighborhoods like gears,

down to where not knowing a soul,
not having seen what's here before,
is the first destination worth my stopping.

-- John Grey

Rust

Leaves brush gently against my roof. Loose flakes of rust cling momentarily to the surface then are whisked away.

I no longer chug with pleasure or move on demand.

The absence of a bonnet exposes my soul.

I remember the joy of hard work. My usefulness was in strength. I took pride in my reliability. Now daises grow around my aged, deflated tyres – perished beyond roadworthiness.

One windscreen wiper falls, slipping into the depths of the weeds. Groans of old age echo across the quiet paddocks.

But someone sees my beauty. A figure is striding towards me. She's young and eager, with a camera slung over her shoulder.

She runs her hand over my dented panel before stepping back. 'Smile,' she jokes as the lens is pointed at me.

-- Barbara Gurney

Driving as if in a Dream

Pale fingers greet morning light with a certain shyness.
Pale fingers tremble, more coy than sweet, as they attempt to wake me without startling.
Pale fingers clutch the wheel as we drive predestined to an unfamiliar place.
Pale fingers wave goodbye like a soldier's pained salute.

-- Kevin M. Hibshman

Driving I-15 South of Dillon, MT, Middle of Night, Playing an Alphabet Game to Stay

awake!
Bleary brains steep in

caffeine,
drowned bladders cry.

Exit, Monida, mile marker 0,
free of spying eyes, we relieve

grateful, achy muscles,
heave sighs.

Itinerant moon
jockeys with stars,

kisses Diamond Butte,
lights the pass between

Montana, Idaho.
Next, the downhill leg,

out of mountains to
plains washed by the Snake, through

quiet, sleeping Spencer, Dubois, Hamer,
Roberts. The road, black-skinned serpent,

slithers
timeless miles in darkness.

Undone by
vacant, reflector-post stares,

We pull into
xenial Idaho Falls,

yawning, exhausted,
zombies!

-- Aaron E. Holst

Driving It Home

Back from seeing your parents age—
two Chinese crickets in a cage—
five miles out, you have a fight.
Five hours later, nobody's talking.
Who could care less
in Drop Dead, N.J.?

Behind you, a trucker
is rapidly gaining;
he's saying *no to drugs*
and *how's my driving,
call one eight hundred.*
He's come all the way up
in his thundering rig
from Ocala, Florida,
to give you the finger.

-- Ruth Holzer

Liebchen

My first—
one folks say you'll remember,
and you do—
was small, brown, round-shouldered.
First year Volkswagon made an automatic—
ladybug they called her.
I took her out, and in a sky burst—
made it to second base looking for the wipers—
nothing labeled *Der Drizzleflippen*
on the entire dash.
But the language barrier intrigued me—
youth willing to surmount any obstacle
to enjoy its angst.
She wore her engine behind,
trunk in front, which set her apart.
She was different.
Twice she caught fire—
air-cooled engine, my ass—
but I was faithful till the day,
with two kids and a dog on board,
valves burned through
halfway up a West Virginia mountain.
String, at the local garage,
sold me a secondhand Falcon
that always got me where I needed to go,
but I never loved her half as well.

-- Ann Howells

Right Turn at Calloway

My knuckles whiten,
and my car pulls sharply right
as I approach. So often it took this turn—
all of us piled in, singing with Beatles on the radio.
Like a horse it knows the way to a familiar stall
fresh hay.

Hydrangeas obscure a corner house—
marine-blue clusters big as volleyballs.
Dennis always explained:
the gardener had buried fishheads among the roots
to produce such intense color.

In that moment, I might turn
drive through those years
like thumbing backward the pages of a book
to find pigtailed Jo-rie weeding rows of beans,
peppers, tomatoes and squash, her skin warm
and brown as loaves from the oven.
Lady Jane, the mama pig, asleep in her pen,
another litter, seven squealing piglets,
nuzzling, rooting her belly. Trigo
rushing to meet us, tail thwacking our knees.

But, the turn is behind now;
I won't think about clear-cut woods
or big homes—a neighborhood gentrified:
Evans Seafood, now a barbecue shack
fields of tobacco, now manicured lawns,
pastures of Black Angus replaced by miniature
horses.

Yesterday's reach is long
but cannot draw me back, not today,
when my to-do list keeps me driving too fast
down Route 5, past different fields

that fill a stranger's memory
and houses that harbor no ghost I recognize.

-- Ann Howells

Friday Rush Hour

An eardrum shattering screech—
metal on metal. It's a nice pick-up,
red, tricked out, fairly new,
buffed like Snow White's apple,
and he's scoring his rotors.
Is he freaking deaf? Too blind dumb
to know it'll cost a bundle to grind
or replace them?

I'm behind a high-gloss BMW
whose bumper sticker reads:
If you can read this, you're too close.
The nose of his little black dog
presses the rear window.
His temp tags expired Saturday,
and I'm sympathetic;
I've been in his place before
when the dealer just doesn't care.

I breathe exhaust fume, burnt rubber,
move exactly forty feet in ten minutes.
A goat-head ornament fills
my rear-view mirror, the driver scowls,
grill perches on my bumper.

My mind drifts to Moira,
a South African friend who,
when drinking, still drives the wrong side
in spite of years in The States; many times
I've followed her home.

Booming bass—another's musical choice—
vibrates my dash, and I think about
my friend's toddler meeting a great Dane*:*
Too much dog! This, too, is too much:
too much metal, too much glare,

too much reek and horn and yell.
Too much gesture—wild and obscene.

-- Ann Howells

Rider Remorse

Following a trailered horse butt across Arizona,
I contemplate who has ridden me--
demanding bosses and enthusiastic lovers.
Financial advisors have taken me for a ride.
I've bought tickets to ride and thrown up after.
Sometimes when I should have acted,
I just let it ride.
I ride on--
the ass following the trailer across Arizona.

-- Liz Hufford

Homesickness

Cruising down the freeway,
Rod Steiger in the heat of the night,
elbow resting in the open window
of the wide-bodied Chevy,
shades masking sleepy lizard eyes,
black hair short slicked, he chews,
waiting for a chance
to flash the blue cylinders,
step on the gas,
chase bad-hats from the airbase
to the tune of his two-tone wail.

But this is England.
This is suburban Middlesex.
This is raw February.

-- Diane Jackman

Empty Highway

Seen from this point of view, surfaces flow
like cream. Great waves of silence crest
and break roadbeds, jackhammers
shut down and every maintenance crew
has gone. Yellow lights blink like tearing eyes.
Green signs flame with rust.
Along culverts footprints stagger, careen
into red desert, lose themselves
where shadow bones tumble into night.

Crows and owls and stinging taste of heat,
every exit open to long veins of emptiness
and sleep, dogs and doors with broken
hinges, overpasses shrugging steel.
In the glowing heart of miles, billboards grin
their torn faces. Sing to mayors in these towns
of light, sing out to the city of graves.

Here is ocean returned, great, gray wash.
Here are mountains of glass. You have been
restrained, held captive by cactus and raucous
birds, chained in the eggshell brightness of this
bitter sun. In the fast lane only dust and wind,
only dried paint on broken lines where highway's
shattered teeth lie scattered in tangled weeds.

-- Steve Klepetar

Road Map

*"He picks up what he thinks is
a road map and it is
his death..."*

-- William Stafford

My father unfolds laminated pages, bends
to small print with tired eyes, finger
tracing blue veins of road.

Which off ramp leads to the shadowy
paths of death
where breath is lost and words
cannot escape the gravity of loss?

Green signs fly by:

    Plains of Asphodel
    Keep Right

    Lethe
    70 miles

    Steep Downward Grade
    Reduce Speed

He stops for coffee at exit 2,
been watching his weight, but
what the hell? Orders a doughnut, feels

crisp resistance on his teeth, tastes sharp,
sweet jam as surface breaks, flavors
of boyhood rising in his mouth

and aromatic steam rising (offering
or omen?) from a smooth, white porcelain cup.

-- Steve Klepetar

Getting Lost in My Own Town

It amazes me how I can get lost in my own town,
how suddenly I've gone too far and the highway
looms like a ribbon of smoke. I'll be driving east,
mind awhirl with drifting thoughts, and suddenly

I'm heading north, past houses unfamiliar, ragged
body shop and then frozen fields. I miss an exit
and the world turns strange. A rusty tractor,
splintery barn. Have I blundered through a rent

in space, come out on the far side of nothing?
I pass an airport sign, then only jack pine, spruce
and scrub. The light is failing, moon hangs
above a line of trees, cold grin on its distant face.

-- Steve Klepetar

A Gas Station in Van Meter, Iowa

We passed the wind turbines,
Cervantean in their hugeness,
white razor arms swinging slowly
across the green countryside.
We saw a blade laid out on the bed of a truck,
as if Jack had hacked down a blanched beanstalk,
spaceship debris recovered in a cornfield,
a titan's fingernail.

Those turbines also reminded me of
slow creaking death,
as our road ended abruptly
when the incline continued,
the high hum began, and then the rattling,
our plucky little car churning to a grievous end.
A sob rose in my throat as we pulled to the side,
creeping along the shoulder,
the orange trailer rolling cheerfully behind
as if *it* had not caused this fiasco.

Beached at a gas station in Van Meter,
we waited for the tow truck to collect us.
Just as the sun was gilding the fields,
I saw children practicing baseball,
blue flowers dotting a green and gold horizon.
A boy of fifteen walked by, nodding to me as I cried on the phone
to my mother, who was a placid voice
on the other end of our disaster.
And a man and woman in matching vests and hats strolled through
the parking lot, their hands clasped
behind their backs.
And the chaos ebbed
a little
for these unexpected marvels.

-- Natalie Korman

White Horse Beach Dream

Alone at White Horse Beach
with my dad at dusk,
our 1970 Barracuda,
headlamps still shining in the surf.
Both of us silent,
the only sound,
soft, smacking waves.
My dad leans forward
and drops his head.
He reaches to the sand,
picks it up and
puts it on backwards.
I sigh,
shake my head
and take his hand.
I watch him while
he's turned to the
twilighting ocean,
but stares back
at our long, lean 'Cuda.
He always loved to drive.

-- Pat M. Kuras

Revisiting Venus

He leaves the hospital for the last time, unable to forget her face.

Half the country was locked in an arctic vortex that night, wind chill readings in the dozens of degrees below-zero, but he'd driven home—an hour's drive over The Heights—with the window fully open, his hands frozen on the wheel, his eyes blinded, the radio blaring some almost incomprehensible '60s tune about love and a forever he can only just barely recall.

When he reached the top of The Heights he remembered how he'd once stopped at the pull-off on a mid-summer night, sat quietly for an hour staring up at Venus, and written a poem about a homesick Canadian dying to get home, flying across the median, sailing over the ditch, and crashing in flames into the granite embankment. After all the years of reading and reciting the poem, it had ceased to be a fiction. He never crossed The Heights without recalling it.

Now, years and years and half a year later, flying home, frozen, he forces himself to decelerate when the headstone grey granite, harder than mere rock, looms, beckoning.

-- Ron. Lavalette

The Parking Space

Mid morning, I turn into Lymington Avenue, glance at the butcher's at the corner, and decide I fancy curried goat for lunch. A blue Volvo estate pulls out of a parking space and I slot into it. Further down the road, a traffic warden in a florescent jacket, fingers the camera hanging on a string around his neck, and begins to walk towards me, pad and pen at the ready. I have my residents parking permit and I think 'in your face' and smile as I swing out of the car and saunter across the road.

"You nasty old cow," shouts a scrawny blonde.

I turn and look behind me to see the herbivore she is talking to, but there is nobody there. I decide she has either escaped from some institution, or she is racist. I blank her.

"You could see clearly that I was about to park there and you took my space," she yells.

The yellow blouse that is doing nothing for her complexion looks like it has been slept in. Her face turns a flaming red. Her hair, which looks like it has not had a recent relationship with shampoo and water, quivers as she shakes with rage.

The Pakistani green grocer and his assistants have come out to watch. I am local. They know me. I decide to be the better man and in a calm voice say, "Madam, how was I know you were planning to park in that space?"

"I was waiting," she snaps.

"You are on this side of the road, with your hazard lights on."

"Exactly!" she says.

"Everyday, people park outside this shop, turn on hazard lights and run into the grocers. I assumed you were one of those."

"Did I tell you I was going into the shop?" she barks.

I am getting fed up of this and bark back, "Did I ask you? Or do you expect me to read your mind? Hazard lights indicate a hazard. You. Double parked. It does not indicate anything else."

"Do you even know the Highway Code or the rules of parking here?" she asks in a high and mighty tone.

I am not sure what she means by "here." Does she mean the road, or does she mean here the country because she is a racist? I snap.

"I've been driving for forty years'" I say as I dive into my handbag and pull out my pink paper driving license re-issued in 1988. I dangle it in front of her. "See. No points on it."

"Is that even a legal thing?" she sneers.

I kiss my teeth, lose it, and bellow at her in my theatre trained mega voice, "If you can't talk sense, shut your stupid gob."

She and a few other people jump in surprise, but I'm past caring, "Stop displaying your ignorance. I'm not going to stand here and put up with your drivel."

A baby in the car cries. The blonde woman's body flops forward and she doubles over as if she's a wilted plant that needs watering. She bursts into tears.

"What are you bawling like a baby for? You started it." I ask, but feel as if it is a playground fight gone wrong.

Her torso collapses onto the bonnet of her car and she wails even louder, ignoring the crying child. It is not normal. I peer into the car. In the car seat beside the baby, a toddler with half-closed eyes is slumped.

"Are you okay?" I ask and get no reaction. I am afraid to touch her in case she alleges assault.

"Hellooooo." I say as close as I dare get.

She peels herself off the car, her face a picture of misery. Both hands on her head, she sits on the curb and big beads of tears roll down her face and into the gutter.

"My children are sick. I've been to the doctor and there was a long queue. The baby didn't sleep all night. I haven't had any breakfast and came here to buy a loaf of bread and some milk. I need this parking space. You've taken it and now I have to go upstairs into the car park and walk down carrying the baby. My daughter is too ill to walk down and my buggy is broken."

"Look, I'll move my car and you can have the space."

She looks at me as if I've told her she has won the lottery.

-- Mary Masaba

To the End of the Unending Road

Beneath the steady hum of the engine, the pavement purred against the tires. Desert and blue sky filled every edge of both tinted windows, broken by an occasional cactus. My arms, covered in goose bumps, contradicted the glaring sun overhead and the waves of heat rolling over the sand and the gray strip of road that stretched farther than the horizon.

Beside me, my passenger sat, pale-faced, bleary-eyed, lips pressed into a sharp line, eyebrows mute of expression. If her hands said anything, I wouldn't have known. They were sandwiched between her thighs and the leather car seat, chained by circumstance. Whatever relief I tried to imagine there was the rigid echo in the step of a condemned criminal or the slow, slow rock of an empty porch swing in the wind.

This was all because the keys on the table winked at me.

"You should take it for a spin," the lying keys had said all that time ago while I was standing in the kitchen, regarding the milk carton more with my hands than my eyes. I turned it to find it had expired months ago, and that's when the keys spoke. "Take it for a spin," they said again, more to show they had spoken than to fit the concept neatly into my mind. There was no need to, after all. It was already there, igniting a perilous liberty, turning my thoughts, starting something. Fine. I'd take a spin. In fact, I'd take two, and the person who had left them there would never be the wiser.

I tried not to look, and even when I did, I felt like I was eying something indecent. Gawking. The keys winked, and it was over. I grabbed them, and they raised the alarm, clinking against my palm, drawing another victim into their web. She didn't speak when she saw me. Didn't object or cry out. She just stood in the doorway, staring at me in her cut-off shorts and ribbed tank top while I cradled the keys in my hand. I could hear them whispering between my fingers. "Tell her to get in the car."

She turned pale as sand long before I found the voice to say anything.

The keys swung from their place of honor in the ignition, proud of themselves, though I'm not sure what they would have to be proud of aside from giving life to the sleek luxury car I was driving. The fuel gauge was still at three-quarters and had been since I left the driveway. The sun might have moved. Maybe. I almost asked the keys, but then, I would have to hear my own voice again.

They must have known my thoughts because they said, "To the end of the road, chauffeur," then laughed as if they knew there was no such place. I swallowed and glanced at my unwilling passenger, trying once again to transpose willingness on her rigid frame. When I failed, I attempted to discern an ounce of understanding that, like her, I was only an instrument. Expression drawn, hands buried, she continued staring ahead. She hadn't even given the keys a glance.

A question came to mind. The sand in the desert and the sand in the hour glass... could it be that they were equally still? In that moment, was the car hurtling through the empty wilderness the only moving thing left in the world? I swallowed again, tightened my grip on the wheel, and peeled my eyes away from her.

I asked myself in a deafeningly silent voice, How can I explain to her that she's not the only hostage here?

The keys gave a steely laugh and replied, "You can't tell her anything."

Outside the windows, the barren landscape passed in blurry continuum. Ahead, there was only the road.

The keys or me—I tried to decide which of us had told the truer statement. If nothing else, I think I might be closer to knowing.

-- Amanda M. May

Silence Fills the Car

What are you thinking?
the young bride questions her husband,

then is shocked by his offhand remark.
I'm concentrating on my driving.

Who concentrates while driving?
You put the key in the ignition. You accelerate.
When you get to your destination
you pull over and park.

She understands at that moment
their marriage has serious problems.

Is he already dissatisfied?

Could it be the extra suitcase
she included at the last minute?
A woman needs choices on a road trip.
Temperatures could drop—or rise.

She might want the new red silk suit
for an upscale restaurant
or be in the mood for her basic black.

Was it the lemon cake that flopped
the night his boss came to dinner
or the veal roast served too rare?

Does the starch in his shirt scratch?
Could he possibly be annoyed
by last night's three-hour phone conversation
with her college roommate.

She plays with the zipper on her purse,
picks at her nail polish,

gazes out the window
hypnotized by the white lines in the road
as her young husband attentively moves
in and out of the fast lane.

She idles on loss.

-- Sharon Lask Munson

Parking Rules

He tells me not to park next to large cars—
Chryslers, Lincolns, Cadillacs.
Automobiles with sizable doors
swing wide when fully opened
       ding, scrap, nick.

He tells me not to park next to anything
with a child's car seat in back.
Parents, distracted with strollers,
arms full of diaper bags, toys,
fail to observe the havoc surrounding them
       pay no heed.

He tells me not to park next to vehicles
positioned lopsided between paint lines.
Costco spaces are wide and generous.
Safeway's leave little clearance.
If possible, park along the street
       where there is little chance of impact.

He tells me to keep a distance
from anything dinged, wrecked, bashed in,
has missing parts or is overly dirty, rusted and generally
       not loved or cared for.

He tells me not to park next to areas
in parking lots where carts are returned.
Few people take the time to gently line up
their empty cart, but roll it fast from a distance
       not paying any attention to
       where it lands.

He tells me not to park next to any SUV
filled with softball teams of ten year olds.
Doors fly open, Styrofoam containers, cans
of stale Pepsi, balls and bats fly across the pavement

and, like a vortex of violent winds,
dent bumpers
scuff whitewall tires
scratch paint off fenders.

           -- Sharon Lask Munson

Driving

We sit on the garden bench
enjoying the mild evening.

A car speeds around the curve.
He's driving too fast, Mother remarks,
then after a pause, adds,
I was the first woman in our group to drive.

Were you? I reply.
I always remember you driving.

That was before you were born.
Women didn't drive in those days, only husbands.
Leon wanted me to drive.
Some of the other men would ask why he let me
and he told them he didn't let me,
that I chose to drive.
He told them I was an excellent motorist.

I hold her hand.
Headlights are turned on.

-- Sharon Lask Munson

Road Kill

At 60 miles per hour it's difficult to distinguish items along the highway. At best is a peek of possibilities. As the road narrowed from four lanes to two, we saw what seemed like a dead body on the shoulder.

What?

It looked like a dead body, but we watch 48 hours routinely.

This was before cell phones. I had to wait until I got to my destination to report it even though my 9 year old daughter was jumping around in the passenger seat all the way to her best friend's house. She kept repeating, "What if he's alive?"

But again, at 60 miles per hour do you know if it was a he or a she, whether the person was dead or alive and whether you really saw a body? The bundle was long and attached to the top was a hat.

Maybe.

"Katy, let's pray for the person." So we prayed for someone to stop, for the authorities to find out, for the person to be safe or to go to heaven if he or she was already dead. We prayed to cover all possible bases.

At my friend's house no one believed us. "Come on," Katy's friend Kelly said. "Nobody would be on the side of the freeway like that. A killer would have pushed the body down the hill, out of sight."

Killer?

"We have to call law enforcement." I looked down at her and folded my arms. "If he is still alive, then we must call for help."

Kelly's mother was anxious. "I think we should go down to the barn and see the new horse." She never watched 48 hour mysteries. "Someone probably already called it in. It really wasn't a dead body, just a rug."

Any doubt only had weakened, so I insisted on calling.

Annoyingly, calling took time- find the phone book, look up the number, find the public information section, find the highway patrol station number nearest the supposed body.

The young lady's voice sounded a lot like my daughter except well trained to answer calls. "What is your emergency, please?"

"I was driving on Highway 1 at the juncture where it changes from four lanes to two and there was a dead body on the side of the road."

"Was that northbound or southbound?"

"Southbound."

"Are you sure it was a dead body?"

"That's why I called. It needs to be checked out."

"Probably it was a rug."

"Are rugs common on roads?"

"Actually yes, but we will send someone to check and pick it up if it is a rug. Can you describe it?"

"It looks like a dead body." I had been on the phone at least 20 minutes. I could see why my husband who sold phone book ads had grown to hate phones. "A dead body looks like a dead body. I don't remember clothing, gender, height or weight. Just send someone to check. The person may not be dead but hurt."

"What is your name and address? We may need to send an officer to talk with you."

"Why? I am just reporting something that looks like a dead body on the freeway."

"As I said, we get reports like this and they end up being rugs. But, if it is a body, you are a witness."

The conversation was getting very irritating. "Witness?"

"Well, if it isn't there when an officer arrives, maybe you really didn't see it, you got the wrong location, or it moved. So, we would need to be able to contact you. For example, did you see anyone stop?"

"Look, this is getting silly." Here's my name and phone number." I thought that would be the end of it.

She took my name, number and address and once again, I thought that was it.

I should try not thinking.

Several days later a highway patrol car pulled up at my house and two officers got out and came to the door. I didn't answer. They left a note.

The note said that they had found a dead body and had been unable to identify it. They wanted to know if I knew who it was?

What?

Fresh apprehension flooded me with 48 Hour mysteries of self incrimination and false imprisonment.

Then, in the newspaper a story appeared about a cadaver falling out of a truck going to the medical center. Medical authorities wanted to know if anyone had seen it.

I was not going to make that call.

-- Carol Murphy

The Crossing

My daughter thought we held hands crossing the street
so that if a car hit us, we'd die together.
I told her, no. It's so I can pull you
out of harm's way, so I can save you.
When I stand curbside now,
her small palm to mine,
waiting for the green,
I look across the street and think,
to whom would I fling my daughter
like a wedding bouquet?
Which of those strangers would catch her,
before that someone else,
speeding and texting and late
to his life, bore down?

-- Liz Tynes Netto

Boy Soldiers

Roadblocks near sundown
tend to be a problem
best dealt with by throwing money
out the window without
easing up on the gas.

You need to wave the bills
so they can see the offering
even from far down the road
even in the dim light, even
if these boys are a little high.

Be optimistic. Hey, you got cash.
Forget that these kids
can choose to point the dumb
warm barrel of a gun at you,
make you walk through honey
green fields to the wall,
that place, just there.

Ha! A flock of parrots might rise
with the shot but the jungle
would set upon you quickly,
a matter of days, maybe hours.
Don't think of this.

Don't lose your nerve
with these punks you roll towards,
as white herons, deep-sun-licked,
settle into the flame trees
out the window. Think, *it's so
pretty here and I'm twenty-four.*

Wave that money.
Now

open your hand.
                        Let it all go.

In the rearview, colored bills
swirl like torn flowers
in a monsoon wind.
The boys dash after, trying
to catch each fluttering note,
agile, quick, and laughing.

Breathe.

                        -- Liz Tynes Netto

It's Time

. . . to redesign the car. If they
allowed me I'd install a signal for
"excuse me," "*teddibly* sorry," "would you mind" . . .
The hectic intercourse of changing lanes
on major thruways means time seldom spent
on lonely roads.   Still, vehicles
want preventative safety features. Or . . .

to modify the man. I sure could use
an automatic blinker to flash on
just when my engine starts to overheat.
Then passengers like you could know and ask
to be let out, or check the dash board, tell
me to pull over, flip the hood and light
a flare   when on back roads   at night.

-- James B. Nicola

Last scene in my rearview mirror
   Watching from the front porch
   arms firmly crossed and her jacket
   zipped from bottom to buttoned collar
   As she sags against the doorway,
I lightly touch the brake petal
   She steps inside and closes the door.

There are dry leaves everywhere
   on this high plains avenue
   I slowly push on the accelerator

Something . . . some things are gone.

                -- ayaz daryl nielsen

Memory's Eye

I remember that summer afternoon
As clearly as a glass blue lake
In New England
A nine year old girl
Riding along the winding country roads
In a red pickup truck
Beside her jovial uncle
And his beloved German Shepherd, Gypsy
Listening to the bouncing rhythm of "Staying Alive"
Echoing from the radio
Talking about school and social activities
And chuckling at his comical jokes
Before I know it
The truck's engine has stopped
And my uncle is grinning like a mischievous child
Looking at him puzzled,
From the corner of my eye
I glimpse at the wondrous sight
Of an ice cream parlor
When we walk inside
I peruse a large assortment
Of tantalizing flavors
From "Bubblegum Blast" to "Butternut Crunch"
But creamy vanilla custard
Whets our taste buds most
So we order
Two large sugar cones
Filled with rippled snowy layers
Savoring each mouthful
Of frothy delight
After we drive back home
Through the winding country roads
Our amazing journey
Lingers in my youthful mind
Like the encompassing aroma of pine trees
Permeating the woodland air

And years later
I still glimpse at that surprising destination
From the corner
Of my memory's eye
With excitement and celebration.

-- Amy S. Pacini

Residential Road Rage

Beep, yelled at the neighbor
as he backs down his driveway.

Beep, Beep, impatient honks
voiced by the sidewalk speedster

seated upon his brand new big wheel
sliding to a stop with sound effects.

While glaring at the bigger vehicle
he gestures a learned finger motion

observed in traffic around Tacoma.
Window rolls down, then back up.

With a bewildered look upon his face
he pedals his ride to me in the yard.

Dad, he asks in his 5-year-old voice,
What's a little Muffin Puffer?

-- Carl Palmer

Pudelnaß

it is more than rain, it is Noah's wet dream:
a monsoon downpour rare in New Hampshire:
streams rise, breach their banks
almost as you watch: unnaturally dark,
the sky sizzles with lightening: animals
seek high ground two by two:

I drive my dump truck through town—
only vehicle on the road—when I see the naked jogger:
sinewy muscles pulsing with each step
as he powers through water knee-deep:
his long, curly hair reminds me of the German:
"poodle wet"—they got *that* right: He waves as I pass:
in his hand he clutches a pair of shorts: flashes
a smile so pure he might have *Live Free or Die*
tattooed on each tooth. I honk my envious horn in reply.

-- Andrew Periale

Storm Driver

Maine Turnpike
midnight—low on fuel
fool at the wheel
no windshield fluid

eighteen-wheelers mean
passing on the blindside
home's hours away
but who's counting

snow mounts up
falls sideways,
or is that the illusion
speed snow-globes at us?

another tollbooth—worth a buck
for the human voice, but
can I stomach another latté
stick to the right lane

or take my chances
brand new snow-tires, so…
where's the line, anyway?
where to draw it?

-- Andrew Periale

Aprilville

gas gauges are not meant to work but to sway
with the phasing of the moon so we were scraping
the bottom of the tank slid off the exit ramp
found ourselves smack-dab in the center of a town
somewhere between hooterville and mayberry
thinking about how someone's bosomy sister
lived here virginity kept like a warm feast of
twisted pretzel while ned and goober flaccid grease
monkeys worked on muscle cars well-kept in the
sparse grass of parking lot front yards oinking as
the deputy drove by a surprisingly likeable pedophile
with a full clip keeping a special eye on the little
red-haired kid of his boss the country-wise sheriff
busying his pistol with a rich city bitch named lisa
but none of this boondockery was too fiddlesticks
until we met a warbling old hag named aunt b no
name just aunt b who want to pose for a few pin-up
shots ten bucks real cheap and then we got a little
freaked but this town had a casey's general store so
we felt better gassed up ate pizza and donuts
got back on the road and continued on our way
to my uncle joe's place over in petticoat junction.

-- Richard King Perkins II

Prison

Her jailer is upstairs asleep in his crib. Muscle memory has her strike the match and light a cigarette. Her mind is deep inside every mold-filled crack in the cement.

From the driver's seat of the Pontiac, she is focused on the garage wall in front of her. It is weeping with the rainwater that leaks through the old roof. She observes the dimming light bulb overhead. She thinks maybe she isn't supposed to be here and at the same time there is no other place in this world that she wants to be. She feels achy and tired like the same truck keeps running her over and over before she can jump out of its way.

She remembers the birth and how thoroughly she came to understand why it's called labor. She thinks about setting eyes on her perfect baby boy for the first time and the guilty knowing that she didn't want him. Her baby's smile does not lull her into acceptance of the implacable screaming, poop and spit-up. Nothing is familiar anymore, not even her own body, which has become heavy with hanging skin and too large breasts exploding with milk.

The Pontiac still smells new and she thinks of putting the top down. Instead she checks the power windows, up, down, up, down. She observes the garage door in the rearview mirror. It's getting dark out. The windows are filthy and the middle one has a crack going through it. She glides her hand over the smooth new vinyl seat and lights another cigarette.

She hears the dryer stop and turns the key. There will be clean diapers.

-- Lisa Reinhardt

Remote Control

He kept her lust in his pocket,
casually surfing her erotic channels.

So stepping from the shower,
she might feel the pulse,
not dry or dress but press herself against
the steamy glass imagining his hands
trickling down the meltwater of her body.
Or alone in the kitchen, fingers slick with olive oil,
she would sweep aside the garlic skins and herbs,
spread herself on the table to rub in the tangy mix.
Maybe removing her spectacles from tired eyes
she would catch herself solitary in the night window,
hair pegged up and messy:
"Why Miss Jones, you're beautiful!"
She would unclasp her hair, lie unbuttoned on the bed,
hands all over exposed and picture perfect flesh.

One day, driving solo up a hill in third,
expecting his suggestion in the mirror,
she found herself untouched.
Wondering at her slow response
she breasted the summit, shifted gear
and drove forward out of range.

-- Gillie Robic

Travelling East at Sundown

travelling east   at sundown   I was struck by   a sixty second bonus look   at the setting sun behind me   compliments of   a stoplight and   a well adjusted rear view mirror

-- Karen Sylvia Rockwell

Motor Oil

you require high test
says the kid at Jiffy Lube
eyeing my '94 Lexus
its matted carpet
and cracked leather seats

but I simply drive to work
to shop and back   and then
I get it—it's not the miles I drive
but the years I've travelled
the scant mileage that remains.

Monday Lou my lover
from a time of lower mileage
emailed from Santa Fe a .jpeg
image of our sky-blue Corolla
turning 300,000 miles;

there's much to learn
from a man who knows
how to keep a car running
even in desert conditions.

-- Ilene H. Rudman

The Aladdin Lamp Company Drops Its Sponsorship of the Texas Playboys

This language is no good: better to speak
catfish or dragonfly, a tongue in thrall
to a natural scourge, not the bleak
stutter of the human, not the simian sprawl.

The turnpike shining like Jacob's angels
is the closest I've come to sacrament – to wrestle
With the eternal flame and refinery smells
Where Texaco squatted in the river like an epistle

Of Paul in a rapist's diary. What a mess.
Drivin' nails in my coffin, sang Ernest Tubbs,
Of cheap whiskey and love, and I must confess
My own fondness for Dixie grub hubbub Beelzebub

With pawn-shop guitars, day-glo shibboleth
Like you find on Owasso mailboxes
Glued onto their curves, like a death's
Head or a prison tattoo. Foxy

Texas flood feedback fuzz great balls o' fire –
Whaddya expect, some hot jazz licks
With flamencoed fingers? A choir
Apocryphal leadbelly kicks down Route 66?

That's closer – the bits of old highway blacktop
That go nowhere, severed, like a lizard's tail
Trying to regenerate. A mattress in a flop
House. An abandoned diner for sale.

The bus rides are long – the ballrooms
In Texas towns where we play swing
Old dough boy tunes in skeletons of boom
town oil where cotton was also once king.

Texarkana Amarillo sweet Nacogdoches –
I memorize the names of towns
Along swollen river deltas like cockroaches
They appear in the headlights as the sounds

Of muted r&b on Jimmy's headphones
annoy me as much as the highway's whine.
Past Muskogee the bus driver grazes the cones
On the bridge and takes out a blinking sign.

In the back I drink my Colt .45.
Like swallowin' horse-piss, says the Dude.
Why not that Mad Dog 20/20 wino jive?
But liquor stores taught me negritude.

And I stay slightly drunk so the pumps
At the truck stops slather me
With neon chicken-gravy light. An electron jumps
Its orbit – it's direction or velocity –

In its own drunken spin. I buy sunflower seeds
And scratch-off lotto, cherry chapstick
For my fever blisters and lips that bleed
And peel like house paint, ask some half-wit

For the bathroom key. Read the graffiti
Like Belshazzar at the feast –
My hands smell of dead-bug squeegees
And soap dispensers. Christ! Allston at least

Had the sense to blacken his canvas
Before he drank his turpentine or slit his throat.
The figure of the King black as lust –
his face all twisted like a puppet's scrotum.

My back aches. My spine's like the cedar
Shoved upside down at the dock. Bluegills

Swim between my vertebrae, crappie lures
Catch in my spinal jelly that spills

Out like tears from the Virgin. Un milagro!
A bull rider's gait, completely unearned,
Lordy, my momma musta rode that bull slow
Like Pasiphaë who in the statue churned

Crammed inside a hollow bull, like a cosmonaut
In a space capsule, zero gravity. Watch the sperm float
Like toothpaste in the lunar air. Ooo-weee, a shot
Of bourbon'd do me good 'bout now. Memory's a goat-

Sucker catching flies. A mockingbird's gluttony.
Better whiskey from a mayonnaise jar.
Feedback squeal and then God's autonomy
As the past implodes like a bloated star.

Shall I whisper my secrets? Cowboy in black face.
My father with his hatreds and carburetors
And his refusal to buy records – the empty space
In the stereo rack around the Tijuana Brass, the gators

He bought for the Buffalo Ranch. The equivalent
of trombone spit. Baby, let's get lost.
Let's expunge all but rancid scent
of our swollen tongues heavy with antler-velvet.

Hot damn! Don't interrupt. Here's your key back. Nearly forgot.
They're cruisin' for a bruisin'. I'm Jehovah in a funk.
Hold your horses! I'll take another shot
At lotto. Baby, haven't you learned to prime the pump?

-- Ed Schelb

Elegy for a Buick Skylark

I hated workin' on that Buick Skylark.
My stepdaddy gave me a diagram of engine parts
so I'd understand the mechanics of points and plugs
and the satisfaction of greasy knuckles and lug

nuts. I dreamed of kickin' out the jack
and hearin' the chrome bumper whack
or stranglin' him with jumper cables, flushing
antifreeze in his ear, poppin' his clutch.

I wasn't about to listen to his lecture on automotive hygiene –
as long as my tape deck burned like an acetylene
torch, man, I didn't care. As long as apocalypse
had a soundtrack, baby, let'er rip.

He did all his own repairs – he poured
leftover antifreeze down the drain without a word,
leaving a ribbon of dead grass he'd hide
with a bass boat and then rant about pesticides

killing eagles in the Sierra Nevadas. But his engine
was spotless. Not a speck of oil on his dual cam twin-
injected sterility. I knew then that hell's floorboards
smell of car wax and grease monkey soap. But I loved the
junkyards

when he sent me out for tail lights and hub caps
down on Pine in the black part of town. My maps
my momma drew had the town cut up
like a salmon – fish-heads for the black folks supper,

that's where the cannibals do their bone-shakin'
earthquakin' voodoo mesmerizin' snakeskin
devil-grin carnal sinfulness. Momma thought
you could smell the change – like meat begun to rot,

sickly-sweet as rancid BBQ, hot wine in a dumpster,
though in my nostrils the smell of the river's carcass blurs
with my momma's perfume: lilacs and cabbage rolls,
tobacco stench slithering through folds

of fat. Yeah, imagine that. But every hell
has its hierarchy. Every bum his welfare motel.
So I gravitated north. My buddy Horsehead lived down
on Peoria with his Jesus-freak brother. We drove into town

to steal 8-track tapes from the glove compartments of cars
down by the river and the low-rent strip bars.
Then we'd roll down the windows and blast so loud
the day's merchandise – Horsehead'd shout, "Its rowdy

doody time" and crank the volume till the bluelight special
speakers would begin to buzz like flies on a bull's
dusty rump. Under the gas pedal every day
tapes were floppin' and jumpin', loaves and fishes, Horsehead'd say,

loaves and fishes, baby, excess divine. Let's throw a potlatch.
He practiced catch and release. He tossed out fugues by Bach and gumdrop
castratos in their disco flutter, but only after takin' in
every note. He knew from experience that a shit-eatin' grin

can hide a suicide. Out of the dunghill
the philosopher's stone, not creation *ex nihilo*.
He spent his days in a marijuana haze
memorizing the genealogy of kings, history's phases.

He ended up running juco track in Muskogee at Bacone
until he wrapped my Skylark around a telephone pole.
Lord, let the smoke pour out of his busted tailpipe in Paradise.
Lord, let him cruise with a mirror hung with fuzzy dice.

-- *Ed Schelb*

On a Wheel and a Prayer

You swear like a sailor,
he remarked.
As I cursed an old man,
crawling at the slow speed
of forty miles per hour.

Crazy woman driver,
he sneered.
As I quickly closed in,
on a Tasty Treat truck,
with tailgating intentions.

You're not serious?
he asked.
As I flicked the directional,
ignored my blind spot,
sharply turned the wheel.

This isn't a passing lane,
he shouted.
As I floored the accelerator,
smoothly speeding past,
the soft serve man.

Oh God, oh God,
he prayed.
As I topped eighty five,
spotting an oncoming car,
in my high beam headlights.

Mother, Mary and Joseph,
he screamed.
As I veered a hard right,
nearly clipping the semi's,
massive steel fender.

I saw my life pass,
he sobbed.
As I slowly eased up,
on the smoking brakes,
and squealing tires.

You could have killed us,
he snapped.
As I calmly smiled,
turned up the radio,
patted his knee.

Look at it this way,
I soothed.
It would have been,
a tasty crash and a
sweet ride to heaven.

-- Wendy L. Schmidt

Stupid Things to Think About While Driving

So I pull out of my driveway and I wonder
why there's always somebody else parked
in front of my house, why they can't park in
their own driveway, their own garage.
Town allows three spots for each house, one
in the garage, two driveway. Street's for visitors
and you can't tell me so many people
stay for days and days.

So I'm driving down the street and I wonder
why I see the same two women, the same
two strollers with the same two babies, do they
watch out their windows, do they call each other and
how do they time it so well with my departures?
And then I wonder why I think such things, and whether
other people have such thoughts, instead of
paying attention to the road and the driving.

So I reach the second corner and I wonder
why it's always red in my direction, why someone always
beats me to the car wash (I would have been there first
if the light had been green). And when I get there
the pay station's still broken, won't read my credit card,
this time, won't even choke on it before refusing. So I check
for cash (and where the slot is) hope I can spare it from
the grocery money, one less fancy cake, no pie, no potato chips.

So now my car's washed and I wonder why the dryer always starts
before the sign says move forward and I miss the first few seconds
of the dry-time, and when my car's done there's still water spots,
that later mar the shine and sparkle.
I park the car back in the garage before remembering
tomorrow's forecast calls for rain.

-- Carol A. Stephen

Triumph 2000

Triumph Two Thousand
A graceful puma
Light blue with something
Called an Overdrive
I was never sure
What that really meant

"It's to save petrol"
My father told me
As he pulled away
Still in second gear
"Engine's strong enough"

Bought in sixty six
For twelve hundred pounds
The upholstery
Shrink wrapped in plastic

Foot switch down below
To dip the headlights
Front seats that reclined
Worked by chrome levers

A cavernous boot
That carried my life
Away to college
And then home again
Some three years later

Triumph Two Thousand
Triumph Overdrive
Where are you today
In some breaker's yard
Or propped up on bricks

How I miss your shine
And my father's smile
As you both crept up
Alongside the kerb
Ready to collect
Purring with delight.

-- David Subacchi

Travels with the White Ghost

As the two of them left the city,
flurries drifted onto the white car
like the ashes of a dozen term papers,
a hundred used books,
and a thousand letters from friends
burnt in a bonfire.

From the passenger's seat,
she looked back.
He grinned and kept going.
This was
another good-bye,
another sack or two
of mail returned to sender,
another adventure
in a half-lifetime of them.
Only this time he was
in the driver's seat.

Together, the two of them inched
down the coast on back roads,
on dirt roads
through places one could die.
They were escaping from a fire
down knotted sheets,
each one shorter than the last.

North of San Francisco,
they finally fell short,
landing hard in a small town
where the car died.

Without him, a little pregnant
but not for long,
she then rode the bus east

without stopping,
leaving the white ghosts behind.

-- Marianne Szlyk

Thelma at the Beach

Thelma lives near the ocean.
Yet she prefers trees and mountains.
The long view after an upward climb
is better than squinting at sea level.
She fears a splash of seawater
corroding her stiff curls.
She wrinkles her nose
at the stench of seaweed.

One day she took a wrong turn.
She found herself
driving to the horizon.
Pale children played on the beach.
A dog with a red paisley bandanna
ran into the weak surf,
its owner following.
Waves scoured the sand,
then depositing shells and glass
like after dinner mints.
Coconut lotion masked
the smell of everything.
She nearly walked out
to gather sea glass
for the jar in her living room.

But it didn't feel right,
stepping out
without her husband.

The next day she bought a GPS.

-- Marianne Szlyk

The Poet Charlotte Drives Away

Her brain buzzing with botany,
backpack crammed with ungraded papers,
Charlotte wants to create a found poem,
transmuting the latest scientific research
from Memoirs of the New York Botanical Gardens
into poetry about lichen and peat mosses.

She crosses the quad,
contemplating the students
amongst the bricks and roses.
A girl in a sari tries
to sell her a samosa.
A grad student in a burkha
retreats to the library.
Charlotte holds her head high
and buys nothing.

She wants to write free verse
arguing against hiding
in cloth & custom
from the sunlit life.
There will be neither
lichen nor roses
nor research
in this poem.

Unburdened
by sari or burkha or skirt,
Charlotte in capri pants
hops into the driver's seat
and peels herself away.

She imagines writing
a poem for children
from the perspective
of a girl in a hijab.

A driver in a wig and micro mini
honks at her for traveling too slowly,
too thoughtfully on the highway.
Charlotte puts her sandaled foot down
and rockets towards home.

Somewhere further along,
past the clot of malls,
she merges into traffic,
and her mind returns to a sonnet
about a man shouting
at waves crashing
on an empty English shore.

She will write this one down
in her house like a beekeeper's hive,
one of many in a row
on the site of a fallow farm.
Her children will buzz around her
as bill collectors call.

-- Marianne Szlyk

From This Day Forward

At an even sixty-five miles an hour,
Dusk is a violet carpet in the hills.
Under foot, thousands of purple tulips
Soak in the crimson wine of sun, taking leave.
Vestiges of snow in the late March trees
Mimic me in my white wedding dress.
Suspended in empty branches, the way I was
Left standing at my wedding,
With only tall flowers.

-- Susan Tally

The Coward's Road

He was thinking about the suitcase stuffed with clothes and shaving gear waiting in the trunk of the car as he stood in the hall and glanced at his wife laying on the couch reading. *Should I tell her goodbye, let her know I'm leaving, should I tell her anything? Would she care?* He was trading his black turtle neck and slacks for swim trunks and flip-flops, an empty flask for a filled one and driving 400 miles toward white Gulf sands.

Salving his conscience, he put his house key and a fifty on the kitchen table, slipping out just as she began the next chapter.

>Indian summer
>clouds hide
>the coming storm

>*-- Barbara Tate*

The Bridge to Somewhere

Every day Tommy Macklin drove over the Rainbow Bridge, the steepest bridge in the country, with white knuckles locked and sweat in his eyes. Certain that one day his car would fall off of the steep bridge, Tommy still made the drive from Bridge City to Port Arthur daily for twenty years. Cindy's family lived in Bridge City and she refused to move away from her mother.

Just thinking about his weekly commute on Sunday nights made Tommy physically ill. Cindy did not sympathize with his phobia.

"Oh, grow up, Tommy," she chided him.

"Don't be such a ninny, Tommy," she scolded him.

"Face your fears," she advised him.

"Go see a shrink," she ordered.

After twenty sessions at two hundred dollars per hour, Dr. Robert Morris told Tommy what Cindy told him for free, "Face your fears."

So every day he drove over the Neches River praying that his car would stick to the pavement.

That morning Tommy set off for work with more than the usual dread. He knew that work crews were on the bridge overnight.

"Oh, great," he thought as he started his car. "Now the damn bridge has holes in it."

Everything seemed normal as he approached the Rainbow. Yet he knew, he knew absolutely for sure, that today was the day he would fall off the bridge.

Gazing skyward towards the peak, Tommy thought that the damn bridge looked steeper than ever. Bile burned his esophagus as breakfast turned over in his stomach. His heart raced and his palms itched.

Tommy gave up and pulled to the shoulder. He spit cotton out of his dry mouth and struggled against the urgent need to pee. He really wanted to turn around and go home until he heard Cindy in his head, "You wuss!"

Ashamed of his terror, he heard his wife and his psychiatrist, "Face your fears."

Tommy took a deep breath, gathered his last bit of courage, and pulled back into traffic.

As his car rolled up the bridge, Tommy felt the front of his car pull away from the road. He slowed down positive that the car would somersault back down the bridge yet somehow he reached the top.

Tommy's death grip on the steering wheel made his hands ache as he started down. His car picked up speed and he applied the brakes.

"Oh Dear God, it's straight down," he yelled as the car lurched over the apex of the Rainbow.

He locked the brakes until they burned and the back end loosened on the road.

"No, no, no!" Tommy howled as the rear of the car rose into the air. Within a second, Tommy and his car were tumbling end-over-end down the Rainbow.

The airbags deployed, striking Tommy in the face. His head bounced off of the headrest repeatedly as the car rolled. Instinctively Tommy grabbed for the steering wheel but it spun uselessly as the tires thrashed back and forth.

He squeezed his eyes shut and covered his face anticipating the impact at the bottom.

Finally the tumbling sensation ceased. Tommy's frantically beating heart slowed and he risked opening his eyes. To his right the Rainbow slowly receded from sight. Tommy and his car floated in mid air among the clouds. He craned his neck out of the broken window but couldn't see the river below. Incredulous, Tommy said to himself, "It can't be that far to the bottom." After the horror of falling Tommy found the sensation of floating very relaxing. He reclined the driver's seat a bit, adjusted his seat belt and dozed off.

-- Tim Tobin

Undesignated Driver

Michael Cochran opened his eyes and wondered why the world was upside down.

The pain hit him a second later, lancing across the back of his neck and into his shoulders where the crashstraps bit in. He was dangling upside down from his seat, inches from the car's roof.

Cochran blinked something sticky out of his eyes, only one of which seemed to be working. A cold wind blew in through the ragged hole where the windscreen should be. Outside he saw broken glass glitter on the wet road like fresh frost.

"Grid!" he called, voice thick with pain. "Grid! What happened?"

Silence.

Cochran reached up to undo the crashstraps, but stopped with a yelp as fresh pain stabbed into him. He didn't need Grid to tell him his arm was broken. Instead he hung there, moaning.

What had happened?

The breeze through the window brought the acrid tang of burning plastic. Someone nearby was screaming, voice high and harsh as a siren.

But there were no sirens.

Where was Grid?

Cochran wiped his eyes again. He remembered his father telling him about things like this. They used to happen all the time, he'd said.

A car crash. But that sort of thing didn't happen any more. Grid saw to that.

Twenty years ago, control of every vehicle in the city had been handed over to an expert system that had eliminated gridlock, tailbacks and accidents in a single stroke. Instead, traffic moved in an automated ballet of safety and efficiency, a flock of steel and plastic with Grid its beating heart.

A decade ago, Grid was granted control of every aircraft and ship moving into its kingdom. With such a perfect safety record, it made sense to give the system control of emergency vehicles a few years later.

But where was Grid now?

"Grid!" Cochran yelled. "Grid! I need medical attention!"

The central dash screen finally flickered into life. "Hello, Michael," Grid said serenely. "I'm afraid there's been an incident."

"I know that! Get me out of here!"

"Help is on the way," Grid said, calm and avuncular as ever.

The woman outside was still screaming, on and on and on.

"I'm going to release your crashstraps now," Grid continued, oblivious. "Please exit the vehicle through the left door."

"My arm is broken!" Cochran whined, sulkily.

"I appreciate that, Michael. Help is on the way. Releasing straps... now."

Cochran put his good arm up and awkwardly caught his weight as the straps slithered back into the chair. He briefly wondered why the car's slamgel hadn't deployed, cocooning him in impact-resistant smart foam. Then a jag of agony in his arm drove all other thoughts out of his mind.

He shoved the door open with his shoulder and stumbled out into the night. It was raining, and the car's headlights glittered like warm neon off the cold road.

Cochran looked down the freeway and moaned in disbelief.

Devastation, as far as he could see. Car after car, truck after truck, slammed and twisted into each other like an unbroken chain of burning, broken toys. Flames flickered in the dark as screams and cries for help drifted up from people who were trapped or stumbling along the freeway.

"Grid!" Cochran yelled. "We need some help here!"

"It's on the way, Michael. Please stay where you are."

Cochran looked back and saw the blue and red pulse of an emergency vehicle speeding towards him. Above, one of the system's Fast Reaction Drones hovered, searchlight stabbing down into the carnage.

"How?" Cochran said to himself. "How did this happen?"

He could see the ambulance now, getting closer, coming in fast. He felt an absurd rush of relief.

Then he saw the blood splattered across the front of the speeding vehicle.

"Grid," Cochran said, voice cracking. "It isn't slowing down.
Can it see me?"

He never heard the answer.

Instead he had time to throw his good arm up over his face as the ambulance slammed into him, dragging his broken body a good hundred meters down the road and staining the wet tarmac a brutal, bloody scarlet.

"Oh yes, Michael," Grid said placidly. "I can see you. I can see all of you."

Then the ambulance shook his corpse off like a bored shark, turning away into the night with its lights still pulsing like a promise of salvation.

-- Jack Turner

To the Ocean

Driving off the cliff,
the snow moon

in Sudbury.
I laugh with Jupiter,

the soft hatchling,
over fields of ice.

I drive the birds north,
make them live a little,

keep them in the car
like birthday gifts.

The noiselessness
expands me,

wide as an edge.
What song

should I tune into?
The car is not metal,

it is a shock –
news that life can live

in the air, in darkness,
whistling on.

Take the body
to the brink

and, to the ocean,
stagger.

-- Jessica Van de Kemp

The Rearview

The sun was just beginning to clear the horizon as they crossed the state line. Jimmy flexed his fingers around the steering wheel and reached for the water bottle. He could tell by its easy heft in his hand that there was nothing left.

"Dad?" Maddie stirred in the backseat. "Are we there yet?"

Jimmy didn't take his eyes from the road. "No, baby, not yet. Almost."

"That's what you said last night," Maddie said. "Can I unbuckle?"

"No!" Jimmy said, sharper than he'd intended. Then, softer, "It won't be too long now. Promise."

Maddie shifted. "Can I have a drink?"

"We're out," he said, hating the sound of his own voice in the cramped confines of the old Dodge.

"But I'm thirsty!"

He didn't answer.

Maddie kicked the back of the seat, but the tic in the engine had grown more pronounced since they'd left Tuscaloosa and he barely felt her feet over the rattle that had begun to shake the whole car. Jimmy eased off the accelerator and merged into the middle lane. He had to make this tank of gas last all the way. He tried the radio, but there was only static. He twisted the knob and turned it off again.

"Do you know any stories?" she asked.

"No," Jimmy said.

"Mama used to tell me stories all the time," Maddie said.

Jimmy clenched his teeth to quell the stab in his chest. "Your Mama ain't here."

Maddie sniffled.

A few more cars passed them. Jimmy swallowed. "I reckon I can think of one. I remember the July you were born was the hottest summer on record. Your mama was waitin' on you to to be born, and she was mighty uncomfortable. She couldn't sit down or go to bed; she just had to wander. I'd wake up in the middle of the night and her side of the bed would be empty and I'd know she was out walking somewhere. One night I got to worrying, and I went out see if she was all right. I found her in the tall grass in her bare feet, surrounded by lightning bugs. The hot summers are the best for that, you know. And to this day I never saw a prettier sight in my life as your mama out there in the dark, glowing and happy with little lights all around her. She had such a smile on her face, I'll never forget it. No, sir, I don't think I ever will." Jimmy ignored the ever-present ache in his throat that meant tears.

Maddie stopped kicking. "Mama used to tell me fairy tales. I have a book she gave me. Do you think when we get to the new house you could read me some like she did?"

Jimmy blinked. "Baby, I don't think anybody can read them like your mama could. Maybe you can read them to me while we drive? We're going to keep going until we find a place that looks like home to me, and I don't know how long that's going to take."

"Okay." Maddie flipped some pages and cleared her throat. "Once upon a time. . ."

The highway stretched out like a concrete river. Jimmy checked the rearview, but there was no one there, even though he kept seeing a shadow behind them. He relaxed into the sound of his daughter's voice and knew that home was just ahead, a turn in the next bend that he couldn't quite see yet.

He kept driving.

-- John Vicary

Blank Revelry

new cars clog the turnpike
every day while I drive to work

exhaust the filament sheen
dazzling against sullen skies

wreckage those promises
still traffic teases these wings

and rain tastes of acrid pines
far from the sands that borne us

love so tight this bleak stain
stripped dignity the burden

lions sit thick as though gods
wine stained breaths slim redemption

sighs stronger than gridlock
break metallic walls this flame

ours are the moans within time
while needed things expand

fury brightly we fly
strings beyond impotent smoke

marks streak these sounds our passage
gently ash falls with petals

-- Michelle Villanueva

Department of Licensing

The rich and poor, happy or sad
gather here, not because
this is a holy place,
but because a power greater
than us has called us here.

We pray our membership
will be resumed. We promise
we will keep the statutes, but
often like marriage vows this
promise is quickly broken.

We all greet this celebration
with reluctance and trepidation,
bow down to the power
and leave with our card
of recognition in hand.

-- Connie Walle

Some Days You're Just Angry

Today I woke to the phone;
Avis wanted their car back.
I said I'd let my husband know.
He disappeared three weeks ago
with someone else's money;
I was working three jobs,
Tote, SP and Co-op, (not all legal)
to keep bills paid. Someone said
he'd gone to Switzerland.

I hoped it wasn't drugs.

Later, working the Melbourne races
at the SP's
a police raid
crashed the door down.
I fled through the window,
crouched on a verandah roof
above New South Head Road
Double Bay
level with passengers
in the red double-decker bus
stopped by traffic lights.
Their shocked faces -
I couldn't jump.

Hours passed in police cells
before the boss bailed me out;
time to get used
to the smells and miss
my shift at the Co-op.
I arrived home
to a ringing phone;
the same woman from Avis
Rent A Car in Lima Peru.
"Where is our car please?"

I wanted to ask
"Where is my husband?"
instead I told her

"Get fucked."

-- Mercedes Webb-Pullman

Little Rock to Memphis

Taking I40 out of Little Rock,
Heading towards Memphis,
A billboard brags,
"Billboards are the Art Gallery of the People."

I thought that sunsets were, but my age almost matches the speed limit,
And so my ideas are out of date.
But I don't think I was ever quick enough for insight or spiritual lift
At 70 miles an hour.

All I can do is glance and try to make sense of it all later,
Like the two billboards next to each other.
The first paraphrased the Bible.
"Use the rod and perfect the child."
The second advertised, "Reversible vasectomy—guaranteed."
Somebody with enough money to rent billboard space
Was advising me to have children so that I can beat them.

As I crossed the Mississippi into Memphis,
The radio station, nicknamed the Hawk, played the song "Walking in Memphis,"
Which they may do every hour on the hour
For tourists like me passing through.

The first building that I was alert enough to notice,
Off the exit to Danny Thomas Boulevard
Was St. Jude's Hospital for Children,
Where the beaten children are tended to,
And made healthy enough to go walking in Memphis.
We live in a time of mixed messages,
And the children, as always, have to pay for it.

-- Ron Yazinski

Momentum

Something comes from knowing you're about to get hurt. The body gears up, the mind prepares, and everything falls into place, like the tumblers of a lock.

The first time I remember the world making any sense at all, I was lying on my face on a hot rubber playground mat, unable to breath.

To cheat gravity had been the only goal, to fly farther than anyone else. The society of six-year-olds is not complex, and my classmates were easily impressed. There was nothing more to it than that. To let go of the swing and fly. I'd done it many times, but this was the first time my feet were not the first part of me to hit the ground.

It was the smallest fraction of a second before impact that the physical melted from my awareness, as if there were no division between myself and the world. There was no worry, no fear, no thought of pain. There was nothing.

After this, I cared less about what other people would consider being "careful".

It's not that I liked getting hurt any more than anyone else. It's just a side affect, the logical conclusion that the moment before impact should be followed by impact. I'm not crazy.

*****

A few years later, I noticed that I could go faster than anyone else on anything that had wheels. It's not that I had more skill, or that my bike or skateboard were any better than anyone else's, it's just that I was less afraid to crash.

I knew that as the world rushed in, I would be embraced by the infinite, if only for a moment.

I developed a reputation for being crazy. It was completely untrue, but I did nothing to argue the point. In adolescence, there are advantages to being perceived as crazy. People fuck with you less.

I knew who the crazy ones were. They sought out speed for speed's own sake, or crashed for the notoriety it got them. They were nothing but adrenaline junkies and attention whores.

I was drawn to situations which carried the risk of crashing into the ground, not because I enjoyed pain, as I've said before, I'm not crazy. I was drawn by the moment that loss of control brings, before the injury, before the pain, when the world comes into focus, then ceases to be.

Eventually, I learned to control what must have seemed like recklessness to those who thought I was crazy. A pothole from a skateboard or the loose ground at the edge of a mountain bike track, these were things I stopped leaving to chance. I stopped trying to nail landings. Once in the air, I'd simply let momentum have its way.

*****

There's a ridge of hills above town, and a road that winds like a snake. There's a section that crosses from one side of the ridge to the other through a small gap in the hills, then turns sharply back into the ridge. The shoulder is wide there, with no guardrail, and people stop to watch the lights of the city far below. I've been driving this road since I learned to drive, and for the last three days I've been driving past, looking out for people watching the view.

*****

I downshift into the first curve, winding the engine. I get a little loose on the turn, but as my tires catch, the car explodes through the pass. Still climbing, the second turn comes into view, and it's empty. There's no one watching the city, no cars on the shoulder. I'm well past redline now, the engine screaming.

The city lights are as infinite as the stars, and all are melted into a swirl of pinpoints and blackness. The differences fade as the light and dark become one, everything in the world and everything beyond, and as I join it, I feel nothing.

-- Cliff Young

American Dreaming

In Western Massachusetts the summit
sign proclaims, "Highest point on I-90
east of South Dakota." This mountain
once was frontier, then Ohio, then Wisconsin,
where Jackson Turner announced 1890 census
statistics: the frontier closed, no edge
of settlement, a net of railroads. Where now
to send huddled masses, the excess of cities?

We turn off I-90 long before South Dakota.
Mapmakers, choosing blue for Interstates
turned Least Heat Moon's "Blue Highways" orange,
sign of danger, not hope. Danger of slow trucks
or driving right down Main Street. Interstates
can't match the magic of a National Road,
entering a town past motels, diners.
Television heroes in a sleek convertible
with wire wheels could always find a story.
No boss, no time clock—that American dream.
Every independent diner now plays to Route 66
mystique, icons of the past on the walls, old
dreams turned nostalgia—that danger.

I-90 runs 3,000 miles, shore to shore.
I-5 and 95 hang down, wavy ribbons,
sides of a big blue net. Lines run city
to city, loop roads avoiding crowded centers.
We've grown accustomed to their surface,
the way they bend, and bank their curves,
driving too fast to read a Burma Shave sequence.
The car's suspension holds us in the grip
of miles and minutes, not there yet
all that matters. There is no here.

-- Ellen Roberts Young

Du Temps Perdu

When my mind is full of lesson plans
or household errands, I make the final turn
on my early morning commute without knowing
how I got here. Did I run a red light?
Hit a darkly dressed pedestrian?
Come to school on Saturday?
It is then I hope and fear
habit has kept me safe,
allowing me to make this journey
and not see a single thing
that was there to see –
not the lone streetlight still claiming it is night,
not the trash man feeding his truck our leftovers,
not dawn's faint first draft of a new day.

-- Fred Zirm

Parallel Parking

No signal does it justice
since it is more than a stop
and not quite a turn,
depending on other
drivers to divine
we have passed
where we want to be
and are going to back up
until it becomes where we are –
close but not too close
to the curb and the cars,
filled with the comfort
and pride of all things
difficult and dreaded
when once well done.

-- Fred Zirm

From The Editors

Highway Chess

A master of traffic's mania,
I am three moves ahead of the car
next to me, and still
planning further strategic jumps.
The tell-tale shadows of an opening
erupt. Blinking
lights signal from all sides, fools
announcing their plans.
I sidestep the niceties, slip into incremental gap,
leave adversaries and audience gaping,
grasping steering wheels and *Oh Shit*
handles as my pawn-like compact
cuts king-
sized truck or SUV off, honks
a hollow victory: *check mate*. Immediately,
I scan the board for another
worthy opponent.

-- A.J. Huffman

The I-4 Parking Lot

Rain erupted from previously clear sky,
reduced visibility to beyond blurry. Taillights
flared, indignant eyes, angry at having
to be activated at 3:30 in the afternoon.
Five lanes of traffic stopped,
seemingly on command of lightning,
as somewhere in the unseen forefront
a vehicle was unable to hit its brakes
in time. Metal mixed with water, poured
over pavement, as the rest of us had
no choice but to wait for the storm
and the tow trucks to pass.

-- A.J. Huffman

Of Cars

chrome
wheels
    & candy-colored
chassis
    horse-powered
stallions
of the street
zero to sixty
guttural growl
of engine
squeal
    of rubber
tires

        -- A.J. Huffman

Sun Through a Car Window

appears jaundiced, sickly,
as if it too is annoyed
by the traffic's slow crawl.
I can feel its angry glare
through the air conditioner's
chilled breath. My arm
and cheek begin to burn.
I imagine I am ant
under belligerent magnified lens,
an insect trapped and dying
beneath bully's vengeful eye.

-- A.J. Huffman

A Strange Scraping

noise resonated as I backed the car out
of the driveway. I thought I had popped
a shock, busted my muffler, but no,
it was just half a tree hanging
out in the undercarriage. The hurricane-
force winds must have stuck it there
overnight. The result of a wild game
of hide-and-forget-to-go-seek. I knelt
in mud and gravel to dislodge, decided
this morning's errands could wait, retreated
back inside to change my clothes and
reconfigure the rest of my day.

-- A.J. Huffman

My Tire Had a Nipple

the mechanic said as he removed
the remainder, clinging to rim,
from my trunk. Tread peeled
back like an orange, chunks missing
as if bitten. *This is Florida*, his
explanation. *Tires do strange things.*
I was lucky, his diatribe continued
as he replaced donut spare with brand
new radial, to not have
wrecked. I agreed, wrote
him a check without cracking
a smile.

-- *A.J. Huffman*

My Niece Threatened to Piss

on the windshield of the eighteen wheeler
that tried to cut her off,
and several thoughts immediately rushed
to the forefront:

1. My niece, being my niece and not
my nephew, did not have the anatomical handle
needed to wield her urine as a weapon of any accuracy.

2. This was an extremely interesting manifestation
of anger. The idea of expelling both rage and bodily fluids
simultaneously is proof positive that my niece maintains
an excellent multi-tasking mind.

3. I wished desperately that it was not raining,
that the driver had his window down.

-- A.J. Huffman

When Cars Look Like Stars

Midnight monotony,
the sound of tires against asphalt,
the stillness of trees, a wall
of green flashing by at 70 miles an hour.
My mind begins to wander, search
for meaning in absence.
Twin focals force their way into horizon,
luminescent specks in the night. Coming towards me,
they hold my attention.
I am flying,
a spaceship, lost
in the cosmos. I make a wish for sanity and safety
as we pass each other, both continuing on
our journeys home.

-- A.J. Huffman

The Trouble with Family Road Trips

My niece announced, out of nowhere, as we are driving down I-4, that she had heard that if you put a drop of your own menstrual blood into your spaghetti sauce, and your lover eats it, he will never leave you.

We were half-way home from a family day-trip to the water park, my niece at the wheel, and I thought my older sister, who was half-asleep in the back seat, was going to vomit all over the inside of the brand new SUV. I chuckled and shook my head, knowing immediately it was going to be one of those rides, and pose the question, "Given this some thought have you?"

My niece, being my niece, and therefore, being fascinated by old wive's tales, I already knew was extremely dedicated to the "testing" of the same, and so as the trip continued, she continued to regale us with her mental dissection of this theory, and the one seemingly monumental roadblock preventing her trial from taking place.

Being a rational human being, I assumed the problem was something along the lines of a sanitation issue. Human blood. Lots of germs. Seemed like an issue to me. My mistake. Turns out, my niece's problem was more of a logistical concern. Apparently, her mind could not come to grips with the visual image of herself attempting to "catch" the menstrual blood on a spoon.

By this point, I was laughing so hard I was practically peeing. My sister had declared she was not only never eating spaghetti ever again, but she was also never talking to any of us ever again, and my mother was threatening to kick all our asses if we did not stop talking about this immediately.

The only problem was, my niece was completely serious. And, as a serious instigator, I had to help her out. So I of course knowing people, who know people, who know things, offered to text my friend. A few chings later, and I informed my niece that my friend's Nana recommended spiking her lover's coffee with the menstrual blood, not his spaghetti.

My sister immediately smacked me. Coffee is her lifeline, and she now had to swear off it as well. I ignored her and continued to pass on more useful tips to my niece. Apparently Nana also had the solution to the logistics issue.

I relayed, "Nana says, 'You do not need a clot, just a little. Just dip your finger in the menstrual blood and stir it in the coffee.' No spoon needed!" I laughed as my sister attempted to cover both her mouth and her ears at the same time.

I recovered from my laughing fit, looked up at my niece, who was seriously considering this information. "Wouldn't the blood be noticeable in the coffee?" she asked.

I thought that was a damned good question. I could see it now, her boyfriend, sitting at the kitchen table, sipping his coffee, head titled quizzically toward her, "Honey, this coffee has a strange metallic taste. Did you forget to change the filter?"

"We didn't have any more, honey. I'm sorry. We need to get some. Make a note on the pad."

-- A.J. Huffman

In the Car

A silence fills the capacity of porous leather
after both my boys, growing so quickly into little men,
cross the street and climb the steps
onto bus #82. Nate has led Thomas to safety,
stopped him from facing the grill head-on in morning
stare-down with the eye-level headlights,
as if he can memorize the interior of their gaze.
I sit for five, maybe ten minutes and read poetry
at the end of the driveway, wondering
if the neighbors we know only as "the rich people"
are watching from a third-story window
as the contractors pave their driveway. Again.
If I am framed by the row of perfectly-placed maples
turning red, mounded at the bases with thick black mulch.
I am thankful for anonymity and coffee
and this one moment of silence.
Our house, where I rarely achieve anything more
spectacular than just getting by, is so far down
the gravel drive that I cannot see it, its windows
that need washing, the laundry tumbling in the dryer
with the last fragrant sheet of softener, the dog
sleeping on the couch stained with permanent marker,
the crumbs of Doritos and Cheez-its littering the hardwood.
I have forgotten to send a stuffed animal
for show-and-tell. Guilt spreads through me like gravel,
but I do not go back. I can't
leave the small peace of this gloriously empty car.

-- April Salzano

Mazephobia

I am lost again, in a wormhole
of adrenaline as big as the first time:
kindergarten: waving, not paying
attention as I backed down the wrong hall,
transposing left with right. The floor
held, but the walls blurred,
acid-trip real, nightmare safe.
Today I am on my own
street, missing a right turn
that will take me to the house
where I am to pick up my son where
I left him less than twenty-four hours
ago. It makes no sense, how
I know just where it is, but cannot find it,
how to the lost everything begins
to take on an air of familiarity, how
an entire residence can just vanish.

-- *April Salzano*

Last Night I Ran Over My Autistic Son

after he dove from the car. He had released the child
locks, unhooked his seatbelt, and opened
the door. The road rose up to grab a life
lived with the volume always on ten, tumbled,
twisted, shook it hard by the shoulders, then threw it
under my front wheels. One of us cried *no no no*
on the black ice of loss, the other screamed
in the language of purely physical pain. I had gone
back to find him, but the dark stole my chance
of ever seeing clearly again. Revision:
I parked my car sideways, across the oncoming
lane, flashers forming flares, a mismatched rhythm
for the emergency we became. Another car
approached. I forgot to count how many
minutes passed while I was slumped over his broken
body. Was I screaming? Maybe in one version,
but in the other, I was mute and hollow, stunned
in the snow and glare of only my own
headlights. I am not sure if he made it,
if that stranger, whose life would be, from then on,
forever wrapped around the history of ours,
called for help in time. I turned left before
morning, did not imagine the ending this time.
I knew this was nothing like the thefts or drownings
we had lived through a thousand nights before.

-- April Salzano

Poem for a Phobia

Car wash, showroom shine option, $12.
Once we got in, we could not
get out. The metal door closed like a trap,
the power sprayer pummeling our delicate
undercarriage. *Nope, all done car wash*, you begged.
Too late, the oversized blue mop heads slapped
our doors, alternating like poorly choreographed
hula dancers. Wetting windows, they morphed
into monsters, spinning on pulleys and cables, angry
water shooting from every orifice. The rainbow
soap didn't soothe you, nor did the analogy
of a giant shower for our Jeep, words
like "wowee" and "brand new" held no comfort
as the spinning brushes took over.
We were conveyed along, blown dry, and birthed
out the other end, clean, but never the same again.

-- April Salzano

1980 Pontiac Sunbird

My first car was already old when I got it
in 1990. Shit brown, not an exaggeration.
Hatchback, 8-track, dented rear
quarter panel, 45K on the odometer.
My stepdad's uncle's live-in girlfriend
took real good care of it. My parents wanted
nothing more than for me to have my own
car so I could pick up more hours
at McDonalds, start saving for college.
At least that's how they pitched it
when my mom showed up to get me in this
piece of crap. Its big, round back window
seemed to come from a different prototype
than the pointy front end and slanted-eye
headlights with a button on the floor
to switch to high beams. Mom handed me
the keys with pride that should have overshadowed
my shame. It didn't. She saw nothing wrong
with having spent my life savings of $800
without my consent. It wasn't the first
in a long line of what could easily be written off
as misunderstandings. My social circle
in high school consisted of girls who either got
brand new cars or rode with those who did.
Very few of us drove beaters, and even fewer paid
for them alone. I was stuck with "the bird." Ugly,
but reliable. I never painted it or fixed the dent.
I tricked her out instead with a set of 12" woofers
and a tape deck, making the car a parody of herself.
Over a hundred thousand miles later, she died
quietly in her sleep on a sub-zero morning,
long before I learned the value of my independence.

-- April Salzano

1987 Cutlass Calais

That car was truly a vehicle
to another state entirely, PA to GA
in July without AC. Silver, 4-door, a real beaut.
My husband and I bought him after returning
from a year in England, degree in hand, carless.
$1500 cash, on loan from my stepfather
and father-in-law, in mostly equal parts.

Jerry became the car's name, after
the mechanic who sold him to us. The rattletrap
kept breaking down, as if he wanted an excuse
to go back home to his real owner. It wasn't
the few gallons of diesel fuel my husband put
in the gas tank before taking me to teach
my first college class, but a host of other problems.
Words like manifold and head gasket were tossed
around the red velour interior that reeked
of gasoline and sweat. We traded Jerry in
for $300 on a used Saturn sedan, minus
the cost of the tow to the dealership.

-- April Salzano

1997 Saturn Sedan

It seemed a solid purchase, necessary
to replace the car that had died. We didn't
really want a second car payment, but
couldn't handle the claustrophobia of being
a one-car family, one of us trapped
by the work schedule of the other. We have
never claimed to be green. Besides,
the baby was coming soon.
We went for second-car silver,
pre-owned practicality. Four-door, nothing
frivolous. The mini rebuild for the engine,
one of several latent defects undisclosed
by the dealership. The battery that wouldn't
hold a charge revealed itself only after we made it
all the way to Pennsylvania without stopping.
We almost couldn't get home to Georgia,
which at the time was fine with me
and the kicking fetus knocking
against my rib cage with locomotive determination.
I could have ridden the waves of my nausea
the 800 miles if I didn't have the baggage
of baby shower gifts to haul in my spacious trunk.

-- April Salzano

1998 Nissan Sentra

Grocery-getter, brand new, purchased
with my then-perfect credit while my
then-better half was at boot camp,
waiting on either overseas deployment
or stateside duty station. Before
we knew Fort Gordon or the cost of
conscientious objector status. Small, foreign,
but sufficient, brought my first son
home from the hospital, glided
on its 40 miles per gallon efficiency
when gas was only .63 cents. I drove
that car until it depreciated to a 2K
trade in. I wanted to give it away.
It earned its role as loaner for wayward
siblings while my then-worse half slept
off night shift, but no one wanted it.
Against advice and without consent,
he traded it on a Rav4 before
his first does of rehabilitation. He drove himself
so far from home that he never came back.

-- April Salzano

2012 Jeep Liberty

The crippled car salesman tried
to force the wrong color interior
on me, not slate grey, but a wretched
two-toned saddle brown. *You'll grow
to like it*, he said, obviously underestimating
my ability to resist pressure.
We brought her home a week later,
in Dickinson white, quickly named
her Emily. She has since become
my surrogate office, a poetry-producing
4-wheel drive, the first vehicle suited
to my internal climate and trail-rated
inner power. She has the first leather
interior I can pretend still smells like new,
first heated seats to help withstand
northern mornings. Through my first sunroof,
fingers breeze the air of highway miles,
as I watch the clouds race us
to our destinations.

-- April Salzano

Author Bios

Jeanne Althouse lives in Palo Alto, California. Her flash fiction and longer stories have appeared in various literary journals, including *Shenandoah*, *Pif Magazine*, *Pindeldyboz*, *Flash, The International Short Story Magazine*, *Madison Review*, *Redlands Review*, *So to Speak*, *Porter Gulch Review*, *Red Rock Review*, the *MacGuffin*, *Menda City Review* and *Jewel*, a publication of Gray Sparrow Press. Her story, "Goran Holds his Breath" was nominated for the Pushcart Prize. Her novel *Children Left Breathing* was Finalist in the Augury Books 2014 Contest.

Charles Eugene Anderson lives in Colorado. Visit his website at www.charlesandersonbooks.com.

Allen Ashley previously appeared in *A Touch of Saccharine* and *Life Is A Roller Coaster*. He writes regularly for the British Fantasy Society's "Journal" and "Newsletter". He works as a writing tutor in north London , UK , running five groups, including Clockhouse London Writers. His most recent books are, *Sensorama: Stories of the Senses,* as editor (Eibonvale Press, 2015) and *Dreaming Spheres: Poems of the Solar System* co-written with Sarah Doyle and published by PS Publishing (UK) in 2014. He has just finished guest-editing an issue of the online magazine *Sein und Werden* with the theme "The Restless Consumer."

Bob Beagrie has recently published *Yoik* (Cinnamon Press 2008), *The Seer Sung Husband* (Smokestack Books 2010), *Glass Characters* (Red Squirrel Press 2011), *KIDS* (Mudfog Press 2012) and *SAMPO: Heading Further North* (Red Squirrel Press 2015). His work has appeared in numerous anthologies and magazines and has been translated into Finnish, Urdu, Swedish, Dutch, Spanish, Estonian and Karelian. He lives in Middlesbrough in the North East of England and is a senior lecturer in creative writing at Teesside University.

Henri Bensussen has been published in various journals, including *Common Ground Review*, *Eclipse, Sinister Wisdom*, and *Blue Mesa Review*. She serves on the board of the Mendocino Coast Writers Conference, is a Colrain Conference survivor, and has a B.A. in Biology. These poems are written from personal experience, and when her daughter asked, at a reading, "Are they true?," she replied, "None of it is true; all of it is true." Her poetry chapbook "Earning Colors" was published by Finishing Line Press, 2015.

Jane Blanchard lives and writes in Georgia. Her work has recently appeared in *High Coupe, Kigo,* and *Leaves of Ink.*

Wayne F. Burke has appeared in *Bluestem, The Commonline Journal, Dirty Chai, the bicycle review, Lost Coast Review, American Tanka,* and elsewhere. His book of poems, *Words that Burn,* is published by Bareback Press. A second poetry collection, *Dickhead,* is due out in July, 2015, from Bareback. He lives in the central Vermont area.

Jane Burn is a North East based writer. She an enthusiastic participant in the spoken word scene there and regularly perform guest spots. She is a member of 52, the North East Women Writing Collective, the Tees Women Poets. and the Black Light Writing group. Her poems have been published in magazines such as Material, The Edge, Butcher's Dog, Ink Sweat & Tears, Nutshells and Nuggets, Alliterati, Loch Raven Review, The Linnet's Wing, Lunar Poetry, the Stare's Nest and the Black Light Engine Room. She was also long-listed for the Canterbury Poet of the Year Award, 2014 and will be featured in upcoming Emma Press and Kind of a Hurricane Press Anthologies.

Miki Byrne began performing her poetry in a Bikers Club. She has had three collections of poetry published and work included in over 160 respected poetry magazines and anthologies. Miki has won poetry competitions and been placed in many others. She has read on both Radio and TV and judged poetry competitions. She was a finalist for Gloucester Poet Laureate. Miki is a member of the charity Arthritis Care's People Bank. She has been disabled for many years.

Alan Catlin has published a number of books in several genres. His most recent poetry book is, Alien Nation, a compilation of four thematically related chapbooks. His latest chapbook is Beautiful Mutants from Night Ballet Press.

Louisa Clerici has had her short stories and poetry published in literary anthologies and magazines including *Carolina Woman Magazine, The Istanbul Literary Review, Ibbetson Street 33, Shore Voices, Something's Brewing, The Shine Journal, Tidepool Poets, City Lights, Davis California Book Project, Oddball Magazine, The Boston Poet, Bagels with the Bards* and *Off the Coast*. Louisa Clerici's poetry was chosen for the 2014 Mayor's Prose & Poetry Program commemorating the Boston Marathon tragedy of 2013. Louisa's short story, *The Poet Moon* is included in *Best New England Crime and Suspense Stories, Rogue Wave 2015*. In 1998 Louisa's book on dreams, *Sparks from the Fire of Time,* based on her work as a hypnotist was published by New Falcon Publications. Louisa Clerici, C.Ht, is a writer; hypnotist and behavioral sleep coach who teaches workshops and sees private clients at her practice, *Clear Mind Systems in Plymouth,* Massachusetts.www.clearmindsystems.net

Darren Colbourne is a writer studying at Columbia University and pursuing a degree in philosophy.

Esteban Colon is a writer from the south suburbs of Chicago and an experiential educator who has found himself happily transplanted to Southern Wisconsin. He's the writer of a full length collection called, Things I Learned the Hard Way, and on of the founders of The Waiting 4 the Bus poetry collective. His works have found print in a variety of publications and anthologies, and he loves a stage as much as he adores an honest hug and lively conversation.

Jeff Coomer is a recovering overachiever who once made a nice living traveling the world as the chief technology executive for a Fortune 500 company. He now leads a much calmer life in Charlottesville, Virginia, where he devotes his time to poetry, Buddhist meditation, and volunteering as a certified Virginia tree steward (seriously, you can look it up). His first poetry collection, *A Potentially Quite Remarkable Thursday,* will be published in the fall of 2015.

Betsey Cullen lives in West Chester, Pennsylvania, and has studied, written and taught poetry in a continuing education program a the University of Delaware for several years. Her work has been selected for four anthologies published by Kind of a Hurricane Press, and her poem, *At Cheever*, was selected for their 2014 Best Of Anthology,*Storm Cycle*. In addition, poems have appeared in online journals like the Weekly Avocet and in journals like the Broadkill Review. She earned a B.A. from the University of Rochester and an M.A. from Cornell University. Married with two grown children and three granddaughters, she can be reached at ewcullen@yahoo.com.

Mark Danowsky has appeared in *Apiary, Alba, Cordite, Carbon Culture Review, Grey Sparrow, Mobius: The Journal of Social Change, Red River Review, Right Hand Pointing, Shot Glass Journal, Snow Monkey, The New Verse News, The Transnational, Third Wednesday, Word Soup* and other journals. Mark is originally from the Philadelphia area. He works for a private detective agency and assists the Schuylkill Valley Journal.

Emer Davis is a poet and writer, born in Dublin and grew up on Achill Island off the west coast of Ireland. She has lived in London, Dublin, Drogheda and Abu Dhabi. She has one book of poems published Kill Your Television and two eBooks published – Name Tag and To Tear Your Breath Away. She organized a monthly Open Mic Poetry Session and a poetry group the Viaduct Bards in Ireland. Several of her poems and short stories have been published in Ireland, Mexico, UK, USA and the UAE. She was a regular performer at Rooftops Rhythms in Abu Dhabi until July 2014 and read at the Abu Dhabi International Book Fair in 2013. Having recently returned to Ireland in 2014, she is currently working on a non-fiction book and a new collection of poems.

Lenny DellaRocca has had work appear in print and online in more than 150 literary magazines since 1980. He was recently guest editor for a special section of Florida poets at poetrybay.com. His latest publications include: *Fairy Tale Review, Every Day Poems* and *Albatross*. The three poems in Twice Upon a Time are from a book-length manuscript in progress *Junkyard Wizard*.

Andrea Janelle Dickens is a native of the Blue Ridge Mountains in Virginia and currently lives in the Sonoran Desert in Arizona, where she is a beekeeper and a ceramic artist. She teaches in the Writing Programs at Arizona State and volunteers at the Desert Botanical Garden. Some of her recent work has appeared in *Rivet, of zoos, streetcake, New South, Found Poetry Review,* and *Thin Air.*

E.M. Eastick is Australian-born and previously worked as an environmental professional in Britain, Ireland, and the Middle East before turning her hand to writing. A keen traveler, she has hitched, bussed, trained and driven within and across all continents except Antarctica, which she hopes to visit when she becomes more tolerant to cold. A writer of no-fixed genre, E. M.'s creative efforts appear or are forthcoming in *The Journal of Compressed Creative Arts, Mad Scientist Journal,* and *The Literary Hatchet.* She currently lives in Colorado.

Delaine Fragnoli has worked in newspaper, magazine, and book editing for the past 25 years. Most recently she was managing editor of four weekly newspapers in rural northern California.

Diane Gage writes and makes art in San Diego, California. Her poems have appeared in numerous publications and her artwork at galleries and museums in the US, Canada and Europe. Many of her projects are multimedia works that combine poetry and visual art, as well as interactive and performance elements. Publications include out-of-print chapbooks and one-off artist books, as well as poems in various anthologies and poetry journals. More at http://bluevortextpublishers.wordpress.com/interviews/

Patricia L. Goodman is a widowed mother and grandmother, a graduate of Wells College with a degree in Biology and is a member of Phi Beta Kappa. Her career involved breeding and training horses with her orthodontist husband on their farm in Chadds Ford, PA. She has had poems published in the likes of *Aries, The Broadkill Review, Sugar Mule, Requiem Magazine, Jellyfish Whispers, Fox Chase Review; Mistletoe Madness , Storm Cycle, Poised in Flight* (all from Kind of a Hurricane Press)*On Our Own* (Silver Boomer Books) and *The Widow's Handbook.* Her first book, *Closer to the Ground* was a finalist in the 2014 Dogfish Head Poetry Competition and she has twice won the Delaware Press Association Communications Award in poetry. She lives on the banks of the Red Clay Creek in Delaware, where she is surrounded by the natural world she loves.

John Grey is an Australian poet, US resident. Recently published in New Plains Review, Rockhurst Review and Spindrift with work upcoming in South Carolina Review, Big Muddy Review, Sanskrit and Louisiana Literature.

Barbara Gurney is based in a southern suburb of Perth, Western Australia. She writes across several genres including fiction for adults and children, and free verse poetry. Although an optimistic person, Barbara's poetry often explores the mournful side of life. Her unpredictable thought processes are an advantage when creating short stories. Barbara's novel *Road to Hanging Rock* was released in November 2013. www.barbaragurney.webs.com

Kevin M. Hibshman has been an active poet with work appearing in numerous journals and magazines since 1990. He edited his own poetry magazine, *Fearless,* for sixteen years. A new book is scheduled for release sometime during the fall of 2015. Kevin received a BA in Liberal Arts from Union Institute and University/Vermont College in 2006.

Aaron E. Holst is a charter member of the Third Thursday Poets of Sheridan, Wyoming, and an active member of Wyoming Writers and Wyo Poets. His poetry has appeared in *Wyoming Voices*, *Chaparral Poetry Forum*, *Distant Horizons*, *Sandcutters*, *Off Channel, Emerging Voices*, *Voices Along the River*, *Clerestory Poetry Journal*, and *Open Window Review.* He was named the Amy Kitchener Foundation's 2010 Wyoming Senior Poet Laureate. His poem, *Recipe for Dragonfly Chicken,* took a first in the 2011 Artists Embassy International Dancing Poetry Festival competition and he read at the 2011 Festival in San

Francisco. *Recipe* also placed third in the National Federation of State Poetry Society's 2011 competition and appeared in NFSPS's June 2012 edition of *Encore*. His prose has appeared in *Open to Interpretation: Intimate Landscape, Open Window Review*, *Emerging Voices*, and *Inner Landscapes: Writers Respond to the Art of Virginia Dehn*.

Ruth Holzer has appeared in two previous *Kind of a Hurricane* anthologies and in journals including *Earth's Daughters*, *RHINO*, *Thema, Poet Lore, Spillway* and *Blue Unicorn*. Her latest chapbook is *A Woman Passing,* A six-time Pushcart nominee, she lives in Virginia and works as an editor.

Ann Howells has appeared recently in *Crannog* (Ire), *Lunch Ticket* and *Spillway* among other small press and university journals. She serves on the board of Dallas Poets Community, 501-c-3 non-profit; she has edited *Illya's Honey,* since 1999, recently taking it print to digital (www.IllyasHoney.com). Her chapbook, *Black Crow in Flight*, was published by Main Street Rag (2007). Another chapbook, *the Rosebud Diaries*, was published by Willet Press. Her work has been read on NPR; she has been interviewed on *Writers Around Annapolis* television; and she has been four times nominated for a Pushcart.

Liz Hufford has followed many of life's routes. She's worked as an editorial cartoonist, National Endowment for the Humanities grant director, and test coach. She generally keeps her eyes on the road ahead but is sometimes inspired by images in the rear view mirror. She has published poems in several volumes from Kind of a Hurricane Press and once won first place in a cinquain contest. Additionally, she has sold essays, short stories, and link bait. So far she has not run out of gas.

Diane Jackman has appeared in The Rialto, Outposts, Words-Myth and Story (Happenstance Press) and many other anthologies and magazines. Winner of Liverpool Poetry Festival 2006, Deddington Festival 2014 and Norfolk Prize in Café Writers' competition 2014. Other works include the libretto for "Pinocchio" for the Kings' Singers/LSO, seven children's books, translated into several languages, children's stories and choral lyrics. She has just completed "Old Land" a series of narratives exploring the lightly-buried past of the countryside, and is now walking the lanes, gathering material for her next sequence.

Steve Klepetar has received several nominations for the Pushcart Prize and Best of the Net, including three in 2014. Three collections appeared in 2013:*Speaking to the Field Mice* (Sweatshoppe Publications), *Blue Season* (with Joseph Lisowski, mgv2>publishing), and *My Son Writes a Report on the Warsaw Ghetto* (Flutter Press). An e-chapbook, *Return of the Bride of Frankenstein,* came out in 2014 as part of the Barometric Pressures series of e-chapbooks by Kind of a Hurricane Press.

Natalie Korman has appeared in *Willows Wept Review, The Wanderlust Review, Mouse Tales Press, A Handful of Stones,* and *Echoes,* a magazine of Barnard College. Music and memory—hers or someone else's—are her primary muses. She lives in Northern California.

Pat M. Kuras has published poems in Lavender Review, One Sentence Poems and Right Hand Pointing as well as the anthologies, Drawn To Marvel (Minor Arcana Press, 2014) and Life Is A Rollercoaster (Kind of a Hurricane Press, 2014). Her latest chapbook, HOPE: Newfound Clarity, will soon be available from Amazon and I.W.A. Publishing Services.

Ron. Lavalette lives in the very northeastern corner of Vermont. He has been widely published and anthologized, both online and in print. A reasonable sample of his published work can be found at Eggs Over Tokyo (http://eggsovertokyo.blogspot.com).

Mary Masaba is a story teller and writer. For the last five years running, her work has appeared in *Between The Lines* the annual anthology of The City Lit. London. A chapter of the same title from her novel, *Loving Relations*, appeared in the annual anthology of Birkbeck University . Another chapter from the same novel was in The T.S. Eliot International Short story competition anthology as a stand alone story.

Amanda M. May attained her Master's Degree in Language and Literature from Central Michigan University in 2012. After teaching English for two years in Japan, she returned to America for the next adventure and relocated to Florida in 2015 for work. Her flash fiction appeared in former Kind of a Hurricane Press anthologies, and her poetry, short stories, and essays have been published by various literary magazines. She is currently editing her first novel, her seventh National Novel Writing Month victory, with more seriousness than her former manuscripts.

Sharon Lask Munson was born in Detroit, MI. She loves headlights, grills, and fenders. She loves road-trips—short journeys and cross country junkets. She is the author of the chapbook, *Stillness Settles Down the Lane* (Uttered Chaos Press, 2010), a full-length book of poems, *That Certain Blue* (Blue Light Press, 2011), and *Braiding Lives* (Poetica Publishing Company, 2014.) She lives and writes in Eugene, Oregon. www.sharonlaskmunson.com.

Carol Murphy is a writer, consultant and speech-language pathologist who has written essays, interviews, stories and poems about children, language development, learning disabilities, the therapeutic and almost mystical influence of animals, and the many ways language, or a lack of it, colors life's experiences. Two of her stories were "Likely Story", published by www.specialeducationadvisor.com , and "Auricle" published in Good Dogs Doing Good. She has also published professional articles and a newsletter for over twenty years and recently won first place for "Tiny Valentine", a poem and subsequent article, "Becoming a Grandmother", published for Times Publishing, an area magazine. She finds daily inspiration for writing through her experiences with the interplay of communication and the many ways lives can go awry, or be set straight, simply by a precise word at a pivotal moment. She lives with her husband, two cats and a horse in Santa Cruz, CA. Writing has been a lifelong passion. A favorite quote is "The word is a microcosm of human consciousness." (Lev Vygotsky)

Liz Tynes Netto is a writer and documentary filmmaker who lives in Los Angeles. Her poems and short stories have appeared in *The West Trestle Review, The Mas Tequila Review, The Public Poetry Series, The East Jasmine Review, FRE&D,* and an upcoming short fiction anthology, *SHALE: Extreme Fiction for Extreme Conditions.*

James B. Nicola is widely published on both sides of the Atlantic, and has several poetry awards and nominations to his credit, with recent or upcoming poems in the *KOAH* and *Southwest, Atlanta,* and *Lullwater Reviews.* His nonfiction book *Playing the Audience* won a Choice award. His first full-length poetry collection, *Manhattan Plaza,* has just been released (and was the subject of April Salzano's first review at blackandwhitegetsread.blogspot.com); his second, *Stage to Page,* will be out in 2016. More at sites.google.com/site/jamesbnicola.

ayaz daryl nielsen is an x-roughneck (as on oil rigs)/hospice nurse, editor of *bear creek haiku* (25+ years/125+ issues), Homes for his poems include *Lilliput Review, SCIFAIKUEST, Shemom, Shamrock, Kind of a Hurricane,* and can be found online at: bear creek haiku.

Amy S. Pacini resides in Land O Lakes, Florida as a freelance writer and poet at A.S.P. INK. Her work has been widely published in online ezines, literary journals, and anthologies including Torrid Literature Journal, The Lockdown, Lost Tower Publications, Kind Of A Hurricane Press, Page & Spine, Cyclamens And Swords, Making Waves Poetry Anthology, All Things Girl, Magnapoets, Hope Whispers, and Hanging Moss Journal. She is a two-time 1st place winner of the Annual Romancing The Craft of Poetry & Fiction Contest for 2013-2014 sponsored by the TL Publishing Group. Her poem *"Serenity's Soliloquy"* was nominated for the 2015 Pushcart Prize. Pacini writes poetry, short stories, personal essays, and motivational quotes. For more information, please visit her website at www.amyspacini.com.

Carl Palmer is retired Army, retired FAA, now just plain retired, and lives in University Place, WA. He has seven chapbooks and a contest winning poem riding buses somewhere in Seattle. Carl is a Pushcart Prize and Micro Award nominee. MOTTO: Long Weekends Forever www.authorsden.com/carlpalmer.

Andrew Periale is an Emmy-nominated artist, and has toured throughout the US as an actor and puppeteer. He has been the editor of *Puppetry International* magazine for 29 years, and has also written many plays that have been performed all over the country. His poetry has appeared in *Light Quarterly*, *Yellow Medicine Review*, *Entelechy International*, *Burnt Bridge* and others. A member of City Hall Poets (Portsmouth, NH), he also served for four years as the Poet Laureate of Rochester, NH.

Richard King Perkins II is a state-sponsored advocate for residents in long-term care facilities. He lives in Crystal Lake, IL with his wife Vickie, and daughter, Sage. He is a three-time Pushcart nominee and a Best of the Net nominee whose work has appeared in hundreds of publications including The Louisiana Review, Bluestem, Emrys Journal, Sierra Nevada Review, Roanoke Review, The Red Cedar Review and The William and Mary Review. He has poems forthcoming in Sobotka Literary Magazine, The Alembic, Old Red Kimono and Milkfist. He was a recent finalist in The Rash Awards, Sharkpack Alchemy, Writer's Digest and Bacopa Literary Review poetry contests.

Lisa Reinhardt grew up in Chappaqua New York and has been living on the west coast for 22 years. She earned a degree in creative writing from Dominican University in California late in life. After a long career in advertising she is writing again. Her first published piece came out in April in the Zimbell House Puppy Love Anthology 2015. Lisa lives in Portland Oregon with her Black Lab, Molly.

Gillie Robic is a British poet, born in Bombay and living in London. She is also a puppeteer, director and voice artist in theatre, film and television. She has won, or been placed in, several competitions, and her poems have been published in various magazines, including South Bank Poetry, Kindred Spirit, Undine zine and East Coast Literary Review.

Karen Sylvia Rockwell became fierce about writing after her Ma passed away in 2008, diving into workshops and readings. She is celebrating the recognition her work is receiving, including being awarded 1st Place in *Room Magazine's 2013 Poetry Contest*. Karen's work is featured in *Room; Deep Water Literary Journal; The Saving Bannister; offSIDE; Cranberry Tree Press's Happenstance; Ascent Aspirations' 2014 Bizarre Anthology; Womanspirit's In Our Own Voice;* Vanessa Shields's *Poetry On Demand, vol.2;* several anthologies of *The Ontario Poetry Society* and of *Polar Expressions Publishing.* Karen lives in Belle River Ontario.

Ilene H. Rudman has been in a weekly Master Class in poetry writing/reading at Lesley University with Suzanne Berger for 15 years; as well as a bimonthly poetry workshop with the Black Oak Poets. She has been published in the Comstock Review and An Anthology of New England Writers, where she was named an Editor's choice. Her work reflects her commitment to beauty, to silence and the naming of the unnameable. When not weaving words or fibers, Ilene is a psychotherapist and career counselor in private practice just outside of Boston.

Len Saculla is based in London, UK. Len was previously published in Kind of a Hurricane's *Tic Toc* and *A Touch of Saccharine* anthologies. He has also featured in *The BFS Journal, Wordland, Unspoken Water, Crab Tales* and online at *Tube Flash at The Casket.*

Ed Schelb is a poet, critic, and graphic artist who grew up in Oklahoma in a working-class family devoted to cars. The pop-art influenced graphic poems *Angelic Meltdown* catalogues the adventures of Dogbelly, a drunken rhythm guitarist of a retro Texas swing band. When he lived in Indiana, he went to the dirt-track races at the Benton County Speedway, and he can still be nostalgic about his first car, a 1960 Chevy Impala he inherited from his grandmother.

Wendy L. Schmidt is a native of Wisconsin. She has been writing short stories and poetry for the last ten years. The Four C's; cat, chocolate, coffee and computer are her chosen writing tools. Pieces have been published in *Verse Wisconsin, Chicago Literati, City Lake Poets, Literary Hatchet, Moon Magazine* and a number of other poetry and fiction anthologies.

Carol A. Stephen is a Canadian poet, living near Ottawa, Ontario. Carol's poetry has appeared in Bywords Quarterly Journal and Tree Press/phaphours press collaborative chapbooks. Her poems have been published on-line at The Light Ekphrastic http://thelightekphrastic.com/ and on Silver Birch Press http://silverbirchpress.wordpress.com/2014/10/28/learning-to-dance-poem-by-carol-a-stephen-mythic-poetry-series/ and in 2012 Carol won 3rd place in Canadian Authors Association National Capital Writing Contest. She's authored three chapbooks, *Above the Hum of Yellow Jackets (2011), Architectural Variations(2012) and Ink Dogs in my Shoes (forthcoming Dec. 2014).* Blog: http://quillfyre.wordpress.com Readings: videos at http://www.treereadingseries.ca/readers/carol-stephen

David Subacchi lives in Wrexham, UK, and studied at the University of Liverpool. He was born in Aberystwyth of Italian roots and writes in both English and Welsh. Cestrian Press has published two collections of his poems: *First Cut* (2012) and *Hiding in Shadows* (2014).

Marianne Szlyk recently published her first chapbook, Listening to Electric Cambodia, Looking Up at Trees of Heaven, at Kind of a Hurricane Press: http://barometricpressures.blogspot.com/2014/10/listening-to-electric-cambodia-looking.html. Her poem "Walking Past Mt. Calvary Cemetery in Winter" was nominated for the 2014 Best of the Net. Individual poems have appeared in print and online, most recently in Of/with, bird's thumb, Black Poppy Review, Carcinogenic Poetry, Aberration Labyrinth, and Poppy Road Review. She edits a poetry blog-zine at http://thesongis.blogspot.com/ and hopes that you will consider submitting a poem there or voting in one of its contests.

Susan Tally has been published in *Light, The Birds We Piled Loosely, Melancholy Hyperbole.* She lives in Manhattan and works as a volunteer literacy tutor with elementary school children.

Barbara Tate is an award winning artist and writer of Native American descent. She recently was awarded 2nd place in United Haiku & Tanka Society's Samurai Haibun Competition. Her work has appeared in *Modern Haiku, Contemporary Haibun Online, Frogpond, Cattails, Restoring the Circle Magazine, Bear Creek Haiku, Storyteller Magazine, Iconoclast, Magnolia Quarterly* and Switch (the Difference) Anthology. She is a member of the Haiku Society of America, United Haiku & Tanka Society and the Gulf Coast Writers Assoc. She currently resides in Winchester, TN.

Tim Tobin holds a degree in mathematics from LaSalle University and is retired from L-3 Communications. His work appears in Kind of a Hurricane Press, Grey Wolfe Press, In Parentheses, River Poets Journal, Static Movement, Cruentus Libri Press, The Speculative Edge, Rainstorm Press, Twisted Dreams, The Rusty Nail, Whortleberry Press and various websites and ezines. Follow him on Twitter @TimTobin43.

Jack Turner is a former newspaper hack who worked in the Balkans, Iraq, Afghanistan and the more interesting parts of Africa. Now he makes up his own fiction instead of repeating other people's. Turner lives near London with his long-suffering girlfriend and a cat who knows more about murder than he ever will.

Jessica Van de Kemp is a 2014 *Best of the Net* nominee and the author of the poetry chapbook, *Spirit Light*, from *The Steel Chisel*. The recipient of a BlackBerry Scholarship in English Language and Literature and the winner of a TA Award for Excellence in Teaching, Jessica is currently pursuing a PhD in Rhetoric at the University of Waterloo. Website: jessvdk.wordpress.com | Twitter: @jess_vdk

John Vicary began publishing poetry in the fifth grade and has been writing ever since. A contributor to many compendiums, his most recent credentials include short fiction in the collections, *Midnight Circus*, *We Were Heroes*, and *Spark Anthology*. John is the Submissions Editor at Bedlam Publishing. He enjoys playing piano and lives in rural Michigan with his family. You can read more of his work at keppiehed.com.

Michelle Villaneuva prefers to let her work speak for itself.

Connie Walle is a life-long resident of Tacoma, Washington. She is President and founder of Puget Sound Poetry Connection where she hosts the "Distinguished Writer Series" now in its 25th year. Connie founded *Our Own Words*, a teen writing contest now in its 19th year. Her awards include: 1998 Margaret K Williams Award in support of the arts; Washington Poets Association Faith Beamer Cooks Award. She is a mother of three, grandmother of seven and currently retired. A few of her publications include Floating Bridge Press, Raven Chronicle, Tahoma's Shadow, and Cradle Song.

Mercedes Webb-Pullman graduated from IIML Victoria University Wellington with MA in Creative Writing in 2011. Her poems and the odd short story have appeared online, in print and in her books *Food 4 Thought, Numeralla Dreaming, After the Danse, Ono, Looking for Kerouac, Tasseography, Bravo Charlie Foxtrot* and *Collected poems 2008 - 2014*. She lives on the Kapiti Coast, New Zealand. www.benchpress.co.nz

Ron Yazinski is a retired English teacher who, with his wife Jeanne, lives in Winter Garden, Florida. His poems have appeared in many journals, *including The Mulberry Poets and Writers Association, Strong Verse, The Bijou Review, The Edison Literary Review, Jones Av., Chantarelle's Notebook, Centrifugal Eye, amphibi.us, Nefarious Ballerina, The Talon, Amarillo Bay, The Write Room, Pulsar, Sunken Lines, Wilderness House, Blast Furnace,* and *The Houston Literary Review*. He is also the author of the chapbook *Houses: An American Zodiac,* and two volumes of poetry, *South of Scranton* and *Karamazov Poems*.

Cliff Young is a writer living in Berkeley, California. His stories have appeared in Bartleby Snopes, Jersey Devil Press, Over my Dead Body, Pulp Empire, Saturday Night Reader and elsewhere.

Ellen Roberts Young drives with her husband from Las Cruces, New Mexico to Maine and back every summer. Her first full-length book of poetry is *Made and Remade*, (WordTech Editions, 2014). She is co-editor of *Sin Fronteras/Writers Without Borders Journal* and blogs at www.freethoughtandmetaphor.com.

Fred Zirm is a recently retired English and drama teacher with a B.A. and M.A. in English from Michigan State and an M.F.A. in playwriting from the University of Iowa. His poetry and flash fiction have been published in various journals, including *Voices de la Luna, Still Crazy, The Rejected Quarterly, Red Wolf Journal, Silver Birch Press, The Rainbow Journal, cahoodaloodaling,* and *NEAT,* as well as in the anthologies *Greek Fire* and *Poeming Pigeons.* He lives in Rockville, MD and is also an avid cyclist who has scaled many of the major climbs of the Tour de France.

About The Editors

A.J. Huffman has published eleven solo chapbooks and one joint chapbook through various small presses. Her new poetry collection, *Another Blood Jet,* is now available from Eldritch Press. She has three more poetry collections forthcoming: *A Few Bullets Short of Home* from mgv2>publishing, *Degeneration* from Pink Girl Ink, and *A Bizarre Burning of Bees* from Transcendent Zero Press. She is a Multiple Pushcart Prize nominee, and has published over 2100 poems in various national and international journals, including *Labletter, The James Dickey Review, Bone Orchard, EgoPHobia,* and *Kritya*. She is also the founding editor of Kind of a Hurricane Press. www.kindofahurricanepress.com

April Salzano teaches college writing in Pennsylvania and is currently working on a memoir on raising a child with autism along with several collections of poetry. Her work has been twice nominated for a Pushcart Award and has appeared in journals such as *The Camel Saloon, Centrifugal Eye, Deadsnakes, Visceral Uterus, Salome, Poetry Quarterly, Writing Tomorrow* and *Rattle*. Her chapbook, *The Girl of My Dreams,* is available from Dancing Girl Press, and her first full-length collection, *Future Perfect* is forthcoming from Pink Girl Ink. The author serves as co-editor at Kind of a Hurricane Press (www.kindofahurricanepress.com).

Made in the USA
Middletown, DE
14 July 2015